cool
food

cool food

LAUREL
GLEN

San Diego, California

Contents

Starters

Hummus with beets

⅓ cup olive oil
1 onion, chopped
16-oz. can beets, drained
1 cup ready-made hummus
2 garlic cloves, crushed
1 tablespoon ground cumin
1–2 tablespoons lemon juice

Heat 1 tablespoon oil in a frying pan, add the onion, and cook for 3 minutes or until soft but not brown.

Place the onion, beets, hummus, garlic, cumin, and lemon juice in a food processor and process the mixture until it is smooth.

Transfer to a serving bowl, season with salt and pepper to taste, and drizzle with the remaining olive oil.

Makes 3 cups

Cheese and chili shapes

1 1/4 cups unbleached flour
pinch of dry hot mustard
6 tablespoons butter, roughly
  chopped
1/2 cup grated cheddar cheese
4 red chilies, seeded and sliced
1 egg yolk

Process the flour, mustard, and butter until they resemble fine breadcrumbs. Add the cheese and chili, then the egg yolk and 1 tablespoon water, and process until the mixture comes together. Gather into a ball, cover with plastic wrap, and refrigerate for 30 minutes.

Preheat the oven to 375°F. On a lightly floured surface, roll out the dough to a 1/4-in. thickness. Cut into 2-in. rounds.

Place on lightly greased cookie sheets and bake for 15–20 minutes or until golden. Allow to cool.

Makes 26

Tzatziki

2 cucumbers
14 oz. plain yogurt
4 garlic cloves, crushed
3 tablespoons finely chopped mint,
  plus extra to garnish
1 tablespoon lemon juice

Cut the cucumbers in half lengthwise. Scoop out the seeds and discard. Leave the skin on and coarsely grate the cucumber into a small colander. Sprinkle with salt and leave over a large bowl for 15 minutes to drain off any bitter juices.

Meanwhile, place the yogurt, crushed garlic, mint, and lemon juice in a bowl and stir until well combined.

Rinse the cucumber under cold water. Then, taking small handfuls, squeeze out any excess moisture. Combine the grated cucumber with the yogurt mixture, then season to taste with salt and freshly ground black pepper. Serve immediately or refrigerate until ready to serve, garnished with the extra mint.

Makes 2 cups

Note: Tzatziki is often served as a dip with flatbread, but is also suitable to serve as a sauce to accompany seafood and meat.
Tzatziki can be stored in an airtight container in the refrigerator for two to three days.

Tahini and chili palmiers

½ cup tahini
1 red chili, seeded and finely chopped
½ teaspoon paprika
2 sheets frozen puff pastry, thawed

Preheat the oven to 400°F. Combine the tahini, chili, and paprika. Spread half the mixture over each sheet of pastry, to the edges.

Fold the pastry from opposite sides until the folds meet in the middle. Then fold one side over the other to resemble a closed book. Refrigerate for 5 minutes to firm.

Cut into ½-in. slices and place on cookie sheets lined with baking parchment, leaving room for spreading.

Bake for 8 minutes, then turn over and bake for 2 minutes or until golden brown.

Makes 36

Cheese fruit log

1/4 cup shelled pistachio nuts
8 oz. cream cheese, softened
1/4 cup finely chopped dried apricots
3 scallions, finely chopped
1/4 cup sun-dried tomatoes, drained
  and finely chopped
1/3 cup finely chopped Italian parsley

Preheat the oven to 400°F. Place the pistachio nuts on a foil-lined baking tray and roast for 5 minutes or until golden brown. Allow to cool, then chop finely.

Beat the cream cheese until smooth. Fold in the apricots, onions, and sun-dried tomatoes; add pepper to taste.

Form the mixture into an 8-in. log. Roll the log in the combined pistachio nuts and parsley. Wrap in plastic wrap and refrigerate until firm.

Makes one 8-in. log

Dolmades

10 oz. grape leaves in brine
¾ cup olive oil
2 onions, finely chopped
¾ cup short-grain rice
6 scallions, finely chopped
⅓ cup chopped dill
1 tablespoon chopped mint
1 tablespoon lemon juice

lemon wedges

Rinse the grape leaves in cold water, soak in warm water for 1 hour, and then drain.

Heat ½ cup of the oil in a large frying pan. Add the onion and cook over low heat for 5 minutes. Remove from the heat, cover, and leave for 5 minutes. Add the rice, scallions, herbs, and lemon juice. Mix well and season.

Lay out a grape leaf, vein-side up, on a plate. Place 3 teaspoons of filling into the center. Fold the sides over the mixture, then roll up toward the tip of the leaf. Repeat until you have made forty-two dolmades.

Use five or six leaves to line the base of a large, heavy-based pan. Pack the dolmades in the lined pan in two layers and drizzle with the remaining oil. Place a plate on top of the dolmades to keep them in place and cover with 1½ cups water. Bring to a boil, reduce the heat, and simmer, covered, for 45 minutes. Remove the plate and lift out the dolmades with a slotted spoon. Serve either warm or cold with the lemon wedges.

Makes 42

Tapenade

$2^2/_3$ cups pitted Kalamata olives
2 garlic cloves, crushed
2 anchovy fillets in oil, drained
2 tablespoons capers in brine, rinsed
  and squeezed dry
2 teaspoons chopped fresh thyme
  leaves
2 teaspoons Dijon mustard
1 tablespoon lemon juice
$1/_4$ cup olive oil
1 tablespoon brand (optional)

Place the Kalamata olives, crushed garlic, anchovies, capers, chopped thyme, Dijon mustard, lemon juice, oil, and brandy in a food processor and process until smooth. Season to taste with salt and freshly ground black pepper. Spoon into a clean, warm jar, cover with a layer of olive oil, seal, and refrigerate for up to one week. Serve on bruschetta or with meze.

Makes $1^1/_2$ cups

Note: To make sure your storage jar is very clean, preheat the oven to 250°F. Wash the jar and lid thoroughly in hot, soapy water or in a dishwasher and rinse well with hot water. Put the jar on a cookie sheet and place in the oven for 20 minutes or until fully dry and you are ready to use it. Do not dry the jar or lid with a towel.

Shrimp san choy bau

36 oz. raw medium shrimp, peeled
and deveined, or 18 oz. raw
shrimp meat
1 tablespoon vegetable oil
1 teaspoon sesame oil
2 scallions, finely chopped
2 garlic cloves, crushed
1 x 1/2 in. piece fresh ginger, peeled
and grated
4 oz. drained water chestnuts,
chopped
1 tablespoon chopped red chili
1 cup cooked white rice
1 cup bean sprouts, trimmed
1/2 cup chopped cilantro
2 tablespoons soy sauce
2 tablespoons oyster sauce
2 tablespoons lime juice
1/4 cup hoisin sauce

Wash the lettuce and separate the
leaves. Shake off any excess water
and drain on paper towels.

If the shrimp are large, cut them into
smaller pieces. Heat a wok over high
heat, add the oils, swirl to coat, then
add the scallions, crushed garlic,
and ginger. Cook for 30 seconds,
then add the shrimp meat, water
chestnuts, and chili. Season with
salt and cracked black pepper and
continue stir-frying for 2 minutes.
Add the cooked rice, bean sprouts,
and cilantro and stir until combined.

Add the soy sauce, oyster sauce, and
lime juice, then remove from the heat.
Transfer the mixture to a serving bowl.
Place the dry lettuce cups on a plate
and spoon the shrimp mixture into
each one. Serve with hoisin sauce.

Serves 4–6

Potato, olive oil, and garlic dip

2 cups mashed potatoes
3 garlic cloves, crushed
3/4 cup olive oil
2 tablespoons white wine vinegar
5 tablespoons milk
1/2 cup chopped fresh herbs

Combine the potatoes and garlic in a bowl. Using an electric beater, gradually beat in half the oil, then the vinegar, then the remaining oil.

Slowly beat in the milk. Add the herbs and season to taste with salt and freshly ground black pepper.

Makes 2 1/2 cups

Flaxseed crackers

1 cup unbleached flour
1/2 teaspoon baking powder
1/2 teaspoon sugar
2 tablespoons flaxseed
1/4 cup milk
2 tablespoons olive oil

Preheat the oven to 400°F. Process the flour, baking powder, sugar, and 1/2 teaspoon salt. Add pepper to taste and stir in the flaxseed. Add the milk and oil and mix to form a wet, crumbly mixture, adding extra milk if the mixture is too dry.

Turn the mixture out onto a flat, lightly floured surface and bring the mixture together into a ball.

Divide the mixture in half, place one half between two sheets of baking parchment, and roll out to a thickness of 1/8 in. Prick liberally with a fork. Cut the dough into twelve irregular triangles and arrange in a single layer on a lightly greased cookie sheet. Repeat with the remaining dough.

Bake for 15–20 minutes or until the bases are lightly golden. Turn over and bake for another 4–5 minutes or until the other side is also lightly golden. Transfer to a wire rack to cool completely.

Makes 24

Falafel

1 cup dried, split fava beans
  (see Note)
1 cup dried chickpeas
1 onion, roughly chopped
6 garlic cloves, roughly chopped
2 teaspoons ground coriander
1 tablespoon ground cumin
½ cup chopped Italian parsley
¼ teaspoon chili powder
½ teaspoon baking soda
3 tablespoons chopped cilantro
vegetable oil for deep-frying

Cover the fava beans with 3 cups water and leave to soak for 48 hours. (Drain the beans, rinse, and cover with fresh water once or twice.) Place the chickpeas in a large bowl, cover with 3 cups water, and soak for 12 hours.

Drain the beans and chickpeas and pat dry with paper towels. Process in a food processor with the onion and garlic until smooth.

Add the ground coriander, cumin, parsley, chili powder, baking soda, and cilantro. Season with salt and pepper and mix until well combined. Transfer to a large bowl, knead, and leave for 30 minutes.

Shape tablespoonfuls of the mixture into balls, flatten slightly, place on a tray, and leave for 20 minutes.

Fill a deep, heavy-based saucepan one-third full of oil and heat to 350°F or until a cube of bread browns in 15 seconds. Cook the falafel in batches for 1–2 minutes or until golden. Drain on paper towels. Serve with hummus, baba ghannouj, and pita bread.

Makes 30

Note: Split fava beans are available from specialty food stores.

Borek

14 oz. feta cheese
2 eggs, lightly beaten
¾ cup chopped Italian parsley
14 oz. phyllo pastry
⅓ cup olive oil

Preheat the oven to 350°F. Lightly grease a cookie sheet. Crumble the feta into a large bowl using a fork or your fingers. Mix in the eggs and parsley and season with freshly ground black pepper.

Cover the phyllo pastry with a damp towel so it doesn't dry out. Remove one sheet at a time. Brushing each sheet lightly with olive oil, layer four sheets on top of one another. Cut the pastry into four 3-in. strips.

Place two rounded teaspoons of the feta mixture in one corner of each strip and fold diagonally, creating a triangle pillow. Place on the cookie sheet, seam-side down, and brush with olive oil. Repeat to make twenty-four pockets. Bake for 20 minutes or until golden. Serve as part of a meze plate.

Makes 24

Note: Fillings for borek are versatile and can be adapted to include your favorite cheeses, such as haloumi, Gruyère, cheddar, or mozzarella.

Gravlax

1 teaspoon crushed black
   peppercorns
¼ cup sugar
2 tablespoons coarse sea salt
5½ lbs. salmon, filleted and boned
   but with the skin left on (ask your
   butcher to do this)
1 tablespoon vodka or brandy
4 tablespoons very finely chopped
   fresh dill

Mustard sauce
1½ tablespoons cider vinegar
1 teaspoon sugar
½ cup olive oil
2 teaspoons chopped fresh dill
2 tablespoons Dijon mustard

Combine the peppercorns, sugar, and salt. Use tweezers to remove any bones from the salmon. Pat dry with paper towels and lay one fillet skin-side down in a tray. Sprinkle with half the vodka, rub half the sugar mixture into the flesh, then sprinkle with half of the dill. Sprinkle the remaining vodka over the second fillet and rub the remaining sugar mixture into the flesh. Lay it flesh-side down on top of the dill-coated salmon. Cover with plastic wrap and place a heavy board on top. Weigh the board down and refrigerate for 24 hours, turning the wrapped fillets over after 12 hours.

To make the mustard sauce, whisk together the vinegar, sugar, oil, dill, and mustard, then cover until needed.

When the salmon is ready, lift off the top fillet and lay both fillets on a board. Brush off the dill and any seasoning mixture with a stiff pastry brush. Sprinkle the fillets with the remaining dill, pressing it onto the salmon, then shake off any excess. Serve the salmon whole, on the serving board. Use a very sharp knife with a flexible blade to thinly slice the salmon at an angle toward the tail and serve with the mustard sauce and dark rye bread.

Serves 20

Roast pepper and eggplant spread

1-lb. eggplant, halved
2 teaspoons olive oil
1 red pepper, halved
2 garlic cloves, crushed
¼ cup chopped mint
3 teaspoons balsamic vinegar

Preheat the oven to 400°F. Brush the cut side of the eggplant with some of the oil. Place cut-side up on a cookie sheet. Brush the skin of the pepper with the remaining oil and place skin-side up on the cookie sheet next to the eggplant. Bake the eggplant and pepper for about 30–35 minutes or until the flesh is soft.

Place the pepper in a plastic bag and leave to cool, then peel away the skin. Allow the eggplant to cool.

Scoop the flesh out of the eggplant and place in a food processor with the pepper, garlic, mint, and balsamic vinegar. Season to taste and process until smooth.

Makes 2 cups

Shrimp pâté with garlic toast

1¼ cups chicken stock
1 tablespoon unflavored powdered
  gelatin
12 oz. cream cheese, at room
  temperature
28 oz. cooked shrimp, peeled,
  deveined, and roughly chopped
2 garlic cloves, crushed
2 tablespoons finely chopped chives
1 tablespoon chopped dill
2 tablespoons butter, melted
2 tablespoons olive oil
1 baguette, cut into ¼-in. slices

Bring a shallow saucepan of water to a boil. Pour the stock into a heatproof bowl, then sprinkle the gelatin evenly over it; do not stir. Remove the saucepan from the heat and place the bowl of chicken stock in the pan. Stir the gelatin into the stock until it has dissolved; remove the bowl and cool for 30 minutes.

Place the gelatin liquid in a blender. Add the cream cheese, half the shrimp meat, and half of the garlic and blend until smooth. Transfer to a bowl and leave for 20 minutes or until thickened slightly.

Add the remaining shrimp meat, chives, and dill and season to taste. Pour into eight ½-cup ramekins. Cover with plastic wrap and refrigerate for 2 hours or until set.

Preheat the oven to 350°F. Combine the butter, oil, and remaining garlic and lightly brush both sides of the bread slices with the mixture. Place the slices on cookie sheets and bake for 10 minutes or until golden and crisp. Leave to cool.

Unmold the pâté and serve with the garlic toast.

Serves 8

Bruschetta

4 Roma tomatoes, chopped
1/3 cup olive oil
1 tablespoon balsamic vinegar
2 tablespoons chopped basil
8 slices day-old, crusty Italian bread
1 garlic clove, peeled

chopped basil, to garnish

Combine the tomatoes, olive oil, balsamic vinegar, and chopped basil. Season well.

Toast the bread on one side. Rub the toasted side lightly with a peeled clove of garlic. Top with the tomato mixture and garnish with the extra chopped basil. Serve immediately.

Makes 8

Crunchy wedges

6 russet potatoes
1 tablespoon vegetable oil
1/4 cup dry breadcrumbs
2 teaspoons chopped chives
1 teaspoon celery salt
1/4 teaspoon garlic powder
1/2 teaspoon chopped rosemary

Preheat the oven to 400°F. Cut the potatoes into eight wedges each and toss in the oil.

Combine the breadcrumbs, chives, celery salt, garlic powder, and rosemary in a bowl. Add the potato wedges and coat well. Place on greased cookie sheets and bake for 40 minutes or until crisp and golden.

Makes 48

Chargrilled baby octopus

2 lbs. baby octopus
3/4 cup red wine
2 tablespoons balsamic vinegar
2 tablespoons soy sauce
2 tablespoons hoisin sauce
1 garlic clove, crushed

Cut off the octopus heads, below the eyes, with a sharp knife. Discard the heads and guts. Push the beaks out with your index finger; remove and discard. Wash the octopus thoroughly under running water and drain on paper towels. If the octopuses are large, cut the tentacles into quarters.

Put the octopus in a large bowl. Stir together the wine, vinegar, soy sauce, hoisin sauce, and garlic in a jar and pour over the octopus. Toss to coat, then cover and refrigerate for several hours or overnight.

Heat a grill or shallow frying pan until very hot and then lightly grease. Drain the octopus, reserving the marinade. Cook in batches for 3–5 minutes or until the octopus flesh turns white. Brush the marinade over the octopus during cooking. Be careful not to overcook or the octopus will be tough. Serve warm or cold. Delicious with a green salad and lime wedges.

Serves 4

Chilled almond soup

1 loaf day-old, white Italian bread,
  crust removed
1 cup whole blanched almonds
3–4 garlic cloves, chopped
1/2 cup extra-virgin olive oil
1/3 cup sherry vinegar or white wine
  vinegar
1 1/4–1 1/2 cups vegetable stock
  or water
2 tablespoons olive oil, extra
1/2 loaf day-old, white Italian bread,
  crust removed, cut into 1/2-in. cubes
1 cup small, seedless green grapes

Soak the bread in cold water for
5 minutes, then squeeze to remove
any excess moisture. Place the
almonds and garlic in a food
processor and process until well
ground. Add the bread and process
to a smooth paste.

With the motor running, add the oil
in a slow, steady stream until the
mixture is the consistency of thick
mayonnaise. Slowly add the sherry
vinegar and 1 1/4 cups of the stock or
water until the mixture has reached
the desired consistency. Blend for
1 minute. Season with salt, then
refrigerate for at least 2 hours. The
soup thickens on refrigeration, so
add more stock or water to reach the
desired consistency.

Heat the extra olive oil in a large frying
pan. Add the bread and toss over
medium heat for 2–3 minutes or
until evenly golden brown. Drain on
crumpled paper towels. Serve the
soup very cold, garnished with the
grapes and bread cubes.

Serves 4–6

Shrimp, mango, and macadamia salad

1 radicchio heart
½ cup basil leaves, torn
1 cup watercress sprigs
24 cooked jumbo shrimp, peeled
    and deveined, with tails intact
3 tablespoons macadamia oil
3 tablespoons extra-virgin olive oil
1 cup macadamia nuts, coarsely
    chopped
2 garlic cloves, crushed
3 tablespoons lemon juice
1 ripe mango, diced

Remove the outer green leaves from the radicchio, leaving only the tender pink leaves. Tear any large leaves in half and arrange in a shallow serving bowl. Sprinkle with half of the basil leaves and the watercress, and toss lightly. Arrange the shrimp over the salad leaves.

Heat the oils in a small frying pan over medium heat. Add the nuts and cook for 5 minutes or until golden. Add the garlic and cook for another 30 seconds, then remove from the heat and add the lemon juice and mango. Season to taste, pour over the salad, and sprinkle with the remaining basil leaves.

Serves 4–6

Pear and walnut salad with blue cheese dressing

Dressing
3½ oz. creamy blue cheese
¼ cup olive oil
1 tablespoon walnut oil
1 tablespoon lemon juice
1 tablespoon cream
2 teaspoons finely chopped sage

1 cup walnut halves
4 firm, ripe, small pears, such as
  Corella
2 tablespoons lemon juice
2 endive heads, trimmed and leaves
  separated
3½ oz. Parmesan cheese, shaved

To make the dressing, puree the blue cheese in a food processor, then add the olive oil, walnut oil, and lemon juice and blend until smooth. With the motor running, slowly add 2 teaspoons warm water. Stir in the cream and sage and season to taste.

Preheat the oven to broil. Place the walnuts in a bowl and cover with boiling water. Allow to steep for 1 minute, then drain. Spread the walnuts on a baking tray and place under the broiler for 3 minutes or until lightly toasted. Chop coarsely.

Thinly slice across the pears through the core to make rounds. Do not peel or core the pears, but discard the seeds. As each pear is sliced, sprinkle with a little lemon juice to prevent discoloration. On each serving plate, arrange three pear slices in a circle. Top with a sprinkling of walnuts, a couple of endive leaves, a few more walnuts, and some Parmesan. Repeat this layering, reserving the last layer of Parmesan and some of the walnuts. Spoon some dressing over each stack, sprinkle with the remaining walnuts, and top each with the reserved Parmesan. Serve as a first course or as an accompaniment to simple meat dishes.

Serves 4

Shrimp with saffron potatoes

16 raw medium shrimp
1/3 cup olive oil
1 lb. new potatoes, cut in half
1/4 teaspoon saffron threads, crushed
1 garlic clove, crushed
1 bird's-eye chili, seeded and finely
  chopped
1 teaspoon grated lime zest
1/4 cup lime juice
7 oz. baby arugula

Preheat the oven to 350°F. Peel and devein the shrimp, leaving the tails intact.

Heat 2 tablespoons of the oil in a frying pan and brown the potatoes. Transfer to a roasting dish and toss gently with the saffron and some salt and black pepper. Bake for 25 minutes or until tender.

Heat a frying pan over medium heat. Toss the shrimp with the garlic, chili, lime zest, and 1 tablespoon of the oil in a small bowl. Grill the shrimp for 2 minutes each side or until pink and cooked.

In a small jar, shake the lime juice and the remaining oil. Season with salt and pepper. Place the potatoes on a plate, top with the arugula and shrimp, and drizzle with dressing.

Serves 4

Salmon carpaccio

3 vine-ripened tomatoes
1 tablespoon baby capers, rinsed
  and drained
1 tablespoon chopped dill
1 lb. sashimi salmon
1 tablespoon extra-virgin olive oil
1 tablespoon lime juice

ciabatta bread

Cut a cross in the base of the tomatoes. Place in a bowl and cover with boiling water. Allow to stand for 2–3 minutes or until the skin blisters. Drain, plunge into cold water, then drain and peel. Cut the tomatoes in half, scoop out the seeds with a teaspoon, and dice the flesh. Place in a bowl and stir in the capers and dill.

Using a very sharp knife, carefully slice the salmon into paper-thin slices, cutting across the grain. Divide the salmon equally among four plates, arranging in a single layer.

Place a mound of the tomato mixture in the center of each plate. Whisk together the olive oil and lime juice and season with salt. Drizzle over the tomato and salmon and season with black pepper. Serve immediately with ciabatta bread.

Serves 4

Artichoke, prosciutto, and arugula salad

4 artichokes
2 eggs, lightly beaten
¼ cup fresh breadcrumbs
¼ cup grated Parmesan cheese
olive oil for frying, plus 1 tablespoon
  extra
8 slices prosciutto
3 teaspoons white wine vinegar
1 garlic clove, crushed
5 oz. arugula, long stalks trimmed

shaved Parmesan cheese (optional)
sea salt

Bring a large saucepan of water to a boil. Remove the hard, outer leaves of each artichoke, trim the stem, and cut 1 in. off the top. Cut into quarters and remove the furry "choke." Boil the pieces for 2 minutes, then drain.

Whisk the eggs in a bowl and combine the seasoned breadcrumbs and grated Parmesan in another bowl. Dip each artichoke quarter into the egg, then roll in the crumb mixture to coat. Fill a frying pan with olive oil to a depth of 1 in. and heat over medium-high heat. Add the artichokes in batches and fry for 2–3 minutes or until golden. Remove from the pan and drain on paper towels.

Heat 1 tablespoon of olive oil in a nonstick frying pan over medium-high heat. Cook the prosciutto in two batches for 2 minutes or until crisp and golden. Remove from the pan, reserving the oil.

Combine the reserved oil, vinegar, and garlic with a little salt and pepper. Place the arugula in a bowl, add half of the salad dressing, and toss well. Divide the arugula, artichokes, and prosciutto among four plates and drizzle with the remaining dressing. Garnish with shaved Parmesan, if desired, and sprinkle with sea salt.

Serves 4

Shrimp mille-feuille

Lemon mayonnaise
1 egg yolk
½ teaspoon Dijon mustard
pinch of sugar
1 teaspoon cider vinegar
1 teaspoon finely grated lemon zest
1 tablespoon lemon juice
¾ cup vegetable oil

2 sheets frozen puff pastry, thawed
1⅔ lbs. cooked medium shrimp
2½ oz. arugula, torn
½ small red onion, thinly sliced
  into rings
2 tablespoons capers, rinsed
  and drained
1 tablespoon chopped Italian parsley

Preheat the oven to 400°F and line two cookie sheets with baking parchment. To make the lemon mayonnaise, combine the egg yolk, mustard, sugar, vinegar, lemon zest, and juice in a bowl. Gradually add the oil, at first drop by drop, then in a thin, steady stream, beating continuously with a whisk or wooden spoon until it thickens. Season to taste.

Cut the pastry sheets into quarters, then place well apart on the cookie sheets. Bake for about 15 minutes or until golden and puffed. Cool for 2 minutes before lifting with a spatula onto a wire rack to cool.

Peel and devein the shrimp, then cut them in half lengthwise. Using half the arugula, shrimp, onion rings, and capers, make a neat pile on four serving plates and drizzle with some of the mayonnaise. Place a piece of pastry over the salad, then add the remaining ingredients, including some mayonnaise, on top of the pastry square. Add another piece of pastry, sprinkle with parsley, and serve.

Serves 4

Haloumi with salad and garlic bread

4 firm, ripe tomatoes
1 cucumber
5 oz. arugula
1/2 cup Kalamata olives
1 loaf crusty white bread, unsliced
5 tablespoons olive oil
1 large garlic clove, cut in half
14 oz. haloumi cheese
1 tablespoon lemon juice
1 tablespoon chopped oregano

Preheat the oven to 350°F. Heat the grill to high.

Cut the tomatoes and cucumber into bite-sized chunks and place in a serving dish with the arugula and olives. Mix well.

Slice the bread into eight 3/4-in. slices, drizzle 1 1/2 tablespoons of the olive oil over the bread, and season with salt and pepper. Grill until lightly golden, then rub each slice thoroughly with a cut side of the garlic. Wrap the bread loosely in foil and keep warm in the oven.

Cut the haloumi into eight slices. Heat 1/2 tablespoon of the oil in a shallow frying pan and fry the haloumi slices for 1–2 minutes on each side, until crisp and golden brown.

Whisk together the lemon juice, oregano, and remaining olive oil to use as a dressing. Season to taste. Pour half the dressing over the salad and toss well. Arrange the haloumi on top and drizzle with the dressing. Serve immediately with the warm garlic bread.

Serves 4

Baked ricotta and red pepper with pesto

1 large red pepper, cut into quarters
  and seeded
26 oz. low-fat ricotta cheese
1 egg
6 slices whole-grain bread

Pesto
2 tablespoons pine nuts
2 cups basil
2 garlic cloves
2 tablespoons good-quality olive oil
2 tablespoons finely grated Parmesan
  cheese

Grill the pepper, skin-side up, under a broiler for 5–6 minutes or until the skin blackens and blisters. Place in a bowl and cover with plastic wrap until cool. Peel off the skin and slice the flesh into 1-in.-wide strips.

To make the pesto, place the pine nuts, basil, and garlic in a food processor and mix for 15 seconds or until finely chopped. While the processor is running, add the oil in a thin, steady stream, then season with salt and pepper. Stir in the Parmesan.

Preheat the oven to 350°F. Grease six large muffin cups.

Mix the ricotta and egg until well combined. Season with salt and freshly ground black pepper. Divide the pepper strips among the muffin cups, top with 2 teaspoons pesto, and spoon in the ricotta mixture.

Bake for 35–40 minutes or until the ricotta is firm and golden. Cool, then unmold. Toast the bread slices and cut them into fingers. Serve with the baked ricotta, with the remaining pesto on the side.

Serves 6

Scallop salad with saffron dressing

pinch saffron threads
1/4 cup mayonnaise
1 1/2 tablespoons cream
1 teaspoon lemon juice
20 scallops (1/2 lb.) with roe attached
2 tablespoons butter
1 tablespoon olive oil
3 1/2 oz. mixed lettuce leaves
1/3 cup chervil leaves

To make the dressing, place the saffron threads in a bowl and soak in 2 teaspoons of hot water for 10 minutes. Add the mayonnaise, mixing well until it is a rich yellow color. Stir in the cream, then the lemon juice. Refrigerate until needed.

Make sure the scallops are clean of digestive tract before cooking. Heat the butter and olive oil in a large frying pan over high heat and sear the scallops in small batches for 1 minute on each side.

Divide the mixed lettuce leaves and chervil among four serving plates, then top each with five scallops. Drizzle the dressing over the scallops and the lettuce leaves before serving.

Serves 4

Orange, goat cheese, and hazelnut salad

1 oz. hazelnuts
1 tablespoon orange juice
1 tablespoon lemon juice
$1/2$ cup olive oil
9 oz. watercress, well rinsed and
dried
2 oz. spinach leaves, well rinsed
and dried
24 orange segments
10 oz. firm goat cheese, sliced into
four equal portions

Preheat the oven to 350°F. Put the hazelnuts on a baking tray and roast for 5–6 minutes or until the skin turns dark brown. Wrap the hazelnuts in a clean towel and rub them together to remove the skins.

Combine the nuts, orange juice, lemon juice, and a pinch of salt in a food processor. With the motor running, gradually add the oil, a few drops at a time. When about half the oil has been added, pour in the remainder in a steady stream.

Remove the stems from the watercress and place the leaves in a bowl with the spinach, orange segments, and 2 tablespoons of the dressing. Toss to combine and season to taste with pepper. Arrange the salad on four plates.

Heat a small, nonstick frying pan over medium-high heat and brush lightly with olive oil. When hot, carefully press each slice of goat cheese firmly into the pan and cook for 1–2 minutes or until a crust has formed on the cheese. Carefully remove the cheese from the pan and arrange over the salads, crust-side up. Drizzle the remaining dressing over the salads.

Serves 4

Shrimp cocktails

Cocktail sauce
1 cup mayonnaise
¼ cup tomato sauce
2 teaspoons Worcestershire sauce
½ teaspoon lemon juice
1 drop hot pepper sauce

2 lbs. cooked medium shrimp

lettuce leaves
lemon wedges
sliced bread

For the cocktail sauce, mix all the ingredients together in a bowl and season with salt and pepper.

Peel the shrimp, leaving some with their tails intact to use as a garnish. Remove the tails from the rest. Gently pull out the dark vein from each shrimp back, starting at the head. Add the shrimp without tails to the sauce and mix to coat.

Arrange lettuce in serving dishes or bowls. Spoon some shrimp into each dish. Garnish with the reserved shrimp, drizzling with some dressing. Serve with lemon wedges and bread.

Serves 6

Note: If you wish, you can make the cocktail sauce several hours ahead and store it in the refrigerator. Stir in 2 tablespoons of heavy cream for a creamier sauce.

Red gazpacho

2 lbs. vine-ripened tomatoes
2 slices day-old, white Italian bread,
  crust removed, broken into pieces
1 red pepper, seeded and roughly
  chopped
2 garlic cloves, chopped
1 small green chili, chopped (optional)
1 teaspoon sugar
2 tablespoons red wine vinegar
2 tablespoons extra-virgin olive oil
8 ice cubes

Garnish
1/2 cucumber, seeded and finely diced
1/2 red pepper, seeded and finely
  diced
1/2 green pepper, seeded and finely
  diced
1/2 red onion, finely diced
1/2 tomato, diced

Score a cross in the base of each tomato. Place in a bowl of boiling water for 1 minute, then plunge into cold water and peel away from the cross. Cut the tomatoes in half, scoop out the seeds, and chop the flesh.

Soak the bread in cold water for 5 minutes, then squeeze out any excess liquid. Place the bread in a food processor with the tomato, pepper, garlic, chili, sugar, and vinegar and process until smooth.

With the motor running, add the oil to make a smooth mixture. Season with salt and ground black pepper. Refrigerate for at least 2 hours. Add a little extra vinegar, if desired.

To make the garnish, place all the ingredients in a bowl and mix well. Serve the soup in bowls with two ice cubes in each bowl. Spoon the garnish into separate bowls.

Serves 4

Scallops, ginger, and spinach salad

10 oz. scallops, without roe
2 cups spinach leaves
1 small red pepper, cut into very
   fine strips
2 oz. bean sprouts
1 fl. oz. sake
1 tablespoon lime juice
2 teaspoons brown sugar
1 teaspoon fish sauce

Remove any membrane or hard white muscle from the scallops. Lightly brush a frying pan with oil. Cook the scallops in batches in the pan for 1 minute each side or until cooked.

Divide the spinach, pepper, and bean sprouts among four plates. Arrange the scallops on the top.

To make the dressing, place the sake, lime juice, brown sugar, and fish sauce in a small bowl and mix together well. Pour over the salad and serve immediately.

Serves 4

Asparagus with smoked salmon and hollandaise

$^3/_4$ cup butter
4 egg yolks
1 tablespoon lime juice
4 eggs, at room temperature
10 oz. asparagus spears
7 oz. smoked salmon
shaved Parmesan cheese

Melt the butter in a small saucepan and skim any froth from the surface. Remove from the heat. In a separate saucepan, mix the egg yolks with 2 tablespoons water. Place over very low heat and whisk for 30 seconds or until pale and foamy, then continue whisking for 2–3 minutes or until the whisk leaves a trail—do not overheat or the eggs will scramble. Remove from the heat. Add the cooled butter a little at a time, whisking well between each addition. Avoid using the milky whey at the bottom of the pan. Stir in the lime juice and season. If the sauce is still runny, return it to the heat and whisk vigorously until thick, being careful not to scramble.

Half-fill a saucepan with water and add the eggs. Bring to a boil and cook for 6–7 minutes, stirring occasionally to center the yolks. Drain and cool, then peel and quarter.

Bring a large saucepan of lightly salted water to a boil. Add the asparagus and cook for 3 minutes or until just tender. Drain and pat dry. Divide the asparagus and smoked salmon among four serving plates. Arrange the eggs over the top. Spoon on the hollandaise and top with the Parmesan. Season and serve.

Serves 4

Haloumi and asparagus salad with salsa verde

9 oz. haloumi cheese
13 oz. small, thin asparagus spears
2 tablespoons garlic oil
1/4 cup basil leaves
1/2 cup mint leaves
1 cup parsley leaves
2 tablespoons baby capers, rinsed
  and drained
1 garlic clove
2 tablespoons olive oil
1 tablespoon lemon juice
1 tablespoon lime juice
2 handfuls mixed salad leaves

Heat a frying pan over medium heat. Cut the haloumi into 1/2-in. slices and cut each slice in half diagonally to make two small triangles. Brush the haloumi and asparagus with the garlic oil. Cook the asparagus for 1 minute or until just tender, and the haloumi until it is warmed through. Keep warm.

To make the salsa verde, place the herbs, capers, garlic, and oil in a food processor and blend until smooth. Add the juices and mix briefly.

Divide the salad leaves among four serving plates. Top with the haloumi and asparagus and drizzle with a little salsa verde.

Serves 4

Sweet citrus scallop salad

Lemon and herb dressing
1/2 preserved lemon
1/4 cup olive oil
2 tablespoons lemon juice
1 tablespoon sweet chili sauce
2 tablespoons white wine vinegar
2 tablespoons chopped cilantro

1 lb. potatoes
vegetable oil, for frying
1 1/2 lbs. scallops, without roe
2 tablespoons olive oil, extra
2 1/2 oz. spinach leaves

For the dressing, scoop out and discard the pulp from the preserved lemon, wash the skin, and cut into thin slices. Put in a bowl and whisk with the olive oil, lemon juice, chili sauce, wine vinegar, and cilantro.

Cut the potatoes into paper-thin slices. Heat 1 in. oil in a deep, heavy-based frying pan and cook batches of the potatoes for 1–2 minutes or until crisp and golden. Drain on crumpled paper towels.

Slice or pull off any membrane, veins, or hard white muscle from the scallops. Heat the extra oil in a frying pan over high heat and cook the scallops in batches for 1–2 minutes or until golden brown on both sides.

Divide half the spinach among four plates. Top with the potatoes, then half the scallops and more spinach. Finish with more scallops. Drizzle with the dressing just before serving.

Serves 4

Smoked salmon and arugula salad

Dressing
1 tablespoon extra-virgin olive oil
2 tablespoons balsamic vinegar

5 oz. arugula
1 avocado
9 oz. smoked salmon
11 oz. marinated goat cheese,
   drained and crumbled
2 tablespoons roasted hazelnuts,
   coarsely chopped

For the dressing, thoroughly whisk together the oil and vinegar in a bowl. Season to taste.

Trim any long stems from the arugula, rinse, pat dry, and gently toss in a bowl with the dressing.

Cut the avocado in half lengthwise, then cut each half lengthwise into six wedges. Discard the skin and place three wedges on each serving plate and arrange a pile of arugula over the top.

Drape pieces of salmon over the arugula. Sprinkle the cheese and nuts over the top and season with ground black pepper. Serve immediately.

Serves 4

Note: A whole smoked trout can be used instead of the salmon. Peel, remove the bones, then break the flesh into bite-sized pieces.

Vietnamese shrimp salad

1 small Chinese cabbage (bok choy),
  finely shredded
$1/4$ cup sugar
$1/4$ cup fish sauce
$1/3$ cup lime juice
1 tablespoon white wine vinegar
1 small red onion, finely sliced
$1 1/2$ lbs. fresh-cooked shrimp, peeled
  and deveined, tails intact
$2/3$ cup chopped cilantro
$2/3$ cup chopped Vietnamese mint
  leaves

Vietnamese mint leaves, extra

Place the cabbage in a large bowl, cover with plastic wrap, and chill for 30 minutes.

Put the sugar, fish sauce, lime juice, vinegar, and $1/2$ teaspoon salt in a small jar and mix well.

Toss together the shredded cabbage, onion, shrimp, cilantro, mint, and dressing and garnish with the extra mint leaves.

Serves 6

Note: Vietnamese mint is available from Asian grocery stores.

Entrées

Lamb with roasted tomatoes

1 tablespoon red wine vinegar
½ small cucumber, finely diced
½ cup plain yogurt
2 teaspoons chopped mint
½ teaspoon ground cumin
⅓ cup olive oil
6 vine-ripened tomatoes
4 garlic cloves, finely chopped
1 tablespoon chopped oregano
1 tablespoon chopped parsley
40 asparagus spears, trimmed
2 lamb fillets (1 lb.)

Combine the vinegar, cucumber, yogurt, chopped mint, cumin, and 1 tablespoon of olive oil.

Preheat the oven to 350°F. Cut the tomatoes in half and scoop out the seeds. Combine the garlic, oregano, and parsley and sprinkle into the tomato shells.

Place the tomatoes on a rack in a roasting pan. Drizzle them with 1 tablespoon of the olive oil and roast for 1 hour. Remove from the oven, cut each piece in half again, and keep warm. Place the asparagus in the roasting pan, drizzle with another tablespoon of olive oil, season, and roast for 10 minutes.

Meanwhile, heat the remaining oil in a frying pan. Season the lamb well and cook over a medium-high heat for 5 minutes on each side, then set aside to cool.

Remove the asparagus from the oven and arrange on a serving plate. Top with the tomatoes. Slice the lamb diagonally and arrange on top of the tomatoes. Drizzle with the dressing and serve immediately.

Serves 4

Indian marinated chicken salad

1/4 cup lemon juice
1 1/2 teaspoons garam masala
1 teaspoon ground turmeric
1 tablespoon finely grated fresh
  ginger
2 garlic cloves, finely chopped
3 1/2 tablespoons vegetable oil
3 boneless, skinless chicken breasts
1 onion, thinly sliced
2 zucchini, thinly sliced diagonally
3 cups watercress leaves
1 cup freshly shelled peas
2 ripe tomatoes, finely chopped
1 cup cilantro

Dressing
1 teaspoon cumin seeds
1/2 teaspoon coriander seeds
1/3 cup plain yogurt
2 tablespoons chopped mint
2 tablespoons lemon juice

Combine the lemon juice, garam masala, turmeric, ginger, garlic, and 2 teaspoons oil in a large bowl. Add the chicken breasts and onion slices, toss to coat in the marinade, cover, and refrigerate for 1 hour.

Remove and discard the onion slices, then heat 2 tablespoons of oil in a large frying pan. Cook the chicken for 4–5 minutes on each side or until it is cooked through. Remove the chicken from the pan and leave for 5 minutes. Cut each breast across the grain into 1/2-in. slices.

Heat the remaining oil in the pan and cook the zucchini for 2 minutes or until lightly golden and tender. Toss with the watercress in a large bowl. Cook the peas in boiling water for 5 minutes or until tender, then drain. Rinse under cold water to cool. Add to the salad with the tomatoes, chicken, and cilantro.

For the dressing, gently roast the cumin and coriander seeds in a dry frying pan for 1–2 minutes or until fragrant. Remove, then pound the seeds to a powder. Mix with the yogurt, mint, and lemon juice, then gently fold through the salad.

Serves 4

White bean salad with tuna

1 cup dried cannellini beans (see
  Note)
2 fresh bay leaves
1 large garlic clove, smashed
$3/4$ lb. green beans, trimmed
2 baby fennel bulbs, thinly sliced
$1/2$ small red onion, very thinly sliced
1 cup parsley leaves, roughly
  chopped
1 tablespoon olive oil
2 fresh tuna fillets (12 oz.)
$1/3$ cup lemon juice
1 garlic clove, extra, finely chopped
1 red chili, seeds removed, finely
  chopped
1 teaspoon sugar
1 tablespoon lemon zest
$1/2$ cup extra-virgin olive oil

Put the cannellini beans in a bowl, cover with cold water, allowing room for the beans to expand, and leave for at least 8 hours.

Rinse the beans well and transfer them to a saucepan. Cover with cold water, add the torn bay leaves and smashed garlic, and simmer for 20–25 minutes or until tender. Drain.

Cook the green beans in boiling water for 1–2 minutes or until tender, and rinse under cold water. Mix with the fennel, onion, and parsley.

Heat the oil in a heavy-bottomed frying pan and cook the tuna fillets over high heat for 2 minutes on each side or until still pink in the center. Remove, cool for 2–3 minutes, then cut into $1 1/4$-in. chunks. Add to the green bean mixture with the cannellini beans and toss to combine.

Combine the lemon juice, garlic, chili, sugar, and lemon zest. Whisk in the olive oil and season with salt and pepper. Toss gently through the salad.

Serves 4–6

Note: You may substitute a 14-oz. can of cooked cannellini beans for the dried beans. Rinse and drain well before using—they will not require any further preparation.

Ground pork and noodle salad

1 tablespoon peanut oil
1 lb. ground pork
2 garlic cloves, finely chopped
1 lemongrass stalk, finely chopped
2–3 red Asian shallots, thinly sliced
3 teaspoons finely grated fresh ginger
1 small red chili, finely chopped
5 fresh kaffir lime leaves, very finely
   shredded
5 oz. mung bean noodles
1 1/3 cups spinach leaves
1 cup roughly chopped cilantro
1 cup peeled, finely chopped fresh
   pineapple
1/2 cup mint leaves
1 1/2 tablespoons brown sugar
2 tablespoons fish sauce
1/3 cup lime juice
2 teaspoons sesame oil
2 teaspoons peanut oil, extra

Heat a wok until very hot, add the peanut oil, and swirl to coat the wok. Add the pork and stir-fry in batches over high heat for 5 minutes or until lightly golden. Add the garlic, lemongrass, shallots, grated ginger, chili, and lime leaves and stir-fry for another 1–2 minutes or until fragrant.

Place the noodles in a large bowl and cover with boiling water for 30 seconds or until softened. Rinse under cold water and drain well. Toss in a bowl with the spinach, cilantro, pineapple, mint, and pork mixture.

To make the dressing, mix together the brown sugar, fish sauce, and lime juice. Add the sesame oil and extra peanut oil and whisk to combine. Toss through the salad and season with freshly ground black pepper.

Serves 4

Warm chicken and pasta salad

12 oz. penne pasta
1/2 cup olive oil
4 long, thin eggplants, thinly sliced
    diagonally
2 boneless, skinless chicken breasts
2 teaspoons lemon juice
1/2 cup chopped Italian parsley
9 oz. roasted red pepper, drained
    and sliced
10 fresh asparagus spears, trimmed,
    blanched, and cut into 2-in. pieces
1/2 cup sun-dried tomatoes, finely
    sliced

grated Parmesan cheese (optional)

Cook the pasta in a large saucepan of boiling water until al dente. Drain, return to the saucepan, and keep warm. Heat 2 tablespoons of the oil in a large frying pan over high heat and cook the eggplants for 4–5 minutes or until golden and cooked through.

Heat a lightly oiled, ridged, cast-iron pan over high heat and cook the chicken for 5 minutes each side or until browned and cooked through. Cut into thick slices. Combine the lemon juice, parsley, and the remaining oil in a small jar and shake well. Return the pasta to the heat, toss through the dressing, chicken, eggplants, pepper slices, asparagus, and tomatoes until well mixed and warmed through. Season with black pepper. Serve warm with a sprinkling of grated Parmesan, if desired.

Serves 4

Greek peppered lamb salad

10 oz. lamb fillets
1½ tablespoons black pepper
3 vine-ripened tomatoes, each cut
   into eight wedges
2 small cucumbers, sliced
¾ cup Kalamata olives, marinated in
   lemon and garlic, drained (reserving
   1½ tablespoons oil)
⅔ cup Greek feta cheese, cubed
¾ teaspoon dried oregano
1 tablespoon lemon juice
1 tablespoon extra-virgin olive oil

Roll the fillets in the pepper, pressing
the pepper on with your fingers.
Cover and refrigerate for 15 minutes.

Place the tomatoes, cucumber, olives,
feta, and ½ teaspoon of the dried
oregano in a bowl.

Heat a ridged, cast-iron pan and
brush with oil. When very hot, cook
the lamb for 2–3 minutes on each
side or until cooked to your liking.
Keep warm.

Whisk the lemon juice, extra-virgin
olive oil, reserved Kalamata oil, and
the remaining dried oregano together
well. Season. Pour half the dressing
over the salad, toss together, and
arrange on a serving platter.

Cut the lamb diagonally into ½-in.-
thick slices and arrange on top of the
salad. Pour the remaining dressing on
top and serve.

Serves 4

Chicken with spinach and raspberries

¼ cup raspberry vinegar
2 tablespoons lime juice
2 garlic cloves, crushed
2 tablespoons chopped oregano
1 teaspoon brown sugar
2 small red chilies, finely chopped
½ cup olive oil
4 boneless, skinless chicken breasts
1 teaspoon Dijon mustard
4 cups spinach leaves
2 cups fresh raspberries

Mix 2 tablespoons of the raspberry vinegar, the lime juice, crushed garlic, 1 tablespoon of the oregano, the sugar, chilies, and ¼ cup of the oil in a large bowl. Immerse the chicken in the marinade, cover, and refrigerate for 2 hours.

Preheat the oven to 350°F. Heat a ridged, cast-iron pan and cook the chicken for 3 minutes on each side, then place on a cookie sheet and bake for another 5 minutes or until cooked through. Allow the chicken to rest for 5 minutes, then cut each breast into five strips diagonally.

To make the dressing, combine the remaining oil, vinegar, and oregano with the mustard, ¼ teaspoon salt, and freshly ground black pepper and mix well. Toss the spinach and raspberries with half of the dressing. Top with the chicken and drizzle with the remaining dressing.

Serves 4

Fusilli salad with sherry vinaigrette

10 oz. fusilli pasta
2 cups cauliflower florets
1/2 cup olive oil
16 slices pancetta
1/2 cup small sage leaves
2/3 cup pine nuts, toasted
2 tablespoons finely chopped Asian
  shallots
1 1/2 tablespoons sherry vinegar
1 small red chili, finely chopped
2 garlic cloves, crushed
1 teaspoon brown sugar
2 tablespoons orange juice
1/4 cup parsley, finely chopped
1/3 cup shaved Parmesan cheese

Cook the fusilli in a large saucepan of rapidly boiling, salted water for 12 minutes or until al dente. Drain and rinse the pasta under cold water until cool. Drain well. Blanch the cauliflower florets in boiling water for 3 minutes, then drain and cool.

Heat 1 tablespoon of olive oil in a nonstick frying pan and cook the pancetta for 2 minutes or until crisp. Drain on crumpled paper towels. Add 1 more tablespoon of oil and cook the sage leaves for 1 minute or until crisp. Drain on crumpled paper towels. In a large serving bowl, combine the pasta, pine nuts, and cauliflower.

Heat the remaining olive oil, add the shallots, and cook gently for 2 minutes or until soft. Remove from the heat, then add the vinegar, chili, garlic, brown sugar, orange juice, and chopped parsley. Pour the warm dressing over the pasta and toss gently to combine.

Place the salad in a serving bowl. Crumble the pancetta over the top and sprinkle with sage leaves and shaved Parmesan. Serve warm.

Serves 6

Shrimp tacos

2 firm, ripe tomatoes, seeded and
  diced
2 tablespoons lime juice
$\frac{1}{2}$ teaspoon chili powder
$\frac{1}{2}$ teaspoon ground cumin
2 tablespoons vegetable oil
1 red onion, diced
4 garlic cloves, crushed
18 medium shrimp, peeled, deveined,
  and roughly chopped
3 tablespoons chopped Italian parsley
8 corn taco shells
5 oz. shredded iceberg lettuce
1 avocado, diced
$\frac{1}{2}$ cup sour cream

Preheat the oven to 350°F. Combine the tomatoes, lime juice, chili powder, and cumin.

Heat the oil in a frying pan, add the onion and garlic, and cook gently for 3–5 minutes or until soft. Add the shrimp and toss briefly, then stir in the tomato mixture and cook for another 3–5 minutes or until the shrimp are pink and cooked. Stir in the parsley. Meanwhile, heat the taco shells on a cookie sheet in the oven for 5 minutes.

Place some lettuce in the bottom of each taco shell, then fill with the shrimp mixture. Top with diced avocado and a dollop of sour cream.

Serves 4

Warm pork salad with blue cheese croutons

1/2 cup olive oil
1 large garlic clove, crushed
12-oz. pork fillet, cut into 1/4-in. slices
1 small or 1/2 large baguette, cut
  into thin slices
3 1/2 oz. blue cheese, crumbled
2 tablespoons sherry vinegar
1/2 teaspoon brown sugar
5 oz. mixed salad leaves

Place the olive oil and garlic in a jar and shake well. Heat 2 teaspoons of the garlic oil in a frying pan, add half the pork, and cook for 1 minute on each side. Remove and keep warm. Add another 2 teaspoons garlic oil and cook the remaining pork. Remove. Season the pork with salt and black pepper to taste.

Lay the bread slices on a cookie sheet and brush with a little garlic oil on one side. Cook the bread under a hot broiler until golden. Turn the bread over, sprinkle with the crumbled blue cheese, then return to the broiler and cook until the cheese has melted (this will happen very quickly).

Add the sherry vinegar and sugar to the remaining garlic oil and shake well. Place the salad leaves in a large bowl, add the pork, and pour the salad dressing on top. Toss well. Place a mound of salad in the middle of each serving plate and arrange five croutons around the edge of each salad. Serve the salad immediately.

Serves 4

Thai beef salad

1¼-lb. beef fillet, trimmed
½ cup fish sauce
1 tablespoon peanut oil
1 small, dried red chili, roughly
  chopped
4 Asian shallots, finely sliced
2 scallions, thinly sliced at an angle
4 tablespoons mint leaves
4 tablespoons cilantro leaves
1 garlic clove, crushed
½ cup lime juice
2 teaspoons brown sugar
2 vine-ripened tomatoes, each cut
  into eight wedges
small head of Bibb lettuce, washed
  and trimmed

Place the beef in a large bowl with 2 tablespoons of fish sauce. Cover and chill for 3 hours, turning the meat several times.

Place a cookie sheet in the oven and preheat to 425°F. Heat the oil in a frying pan over high heat and cook the beef for 1 minute on each side or until browned, then roast for 15 minutes or until medium-rare. Remove from the oven and allow to cool for 10 minutes.

Meanwhile, place the chili in a small, nonstick frying pan over medium-high heat. Dry-fry for 1–2 minutes or until the chili is dark but not burned. Transfer to a mortar and pestle or spice mill and grind until fine. Mix the ground chili in a bowl with the shallots, scallions, mint, cilantro, garlic, lime juice, brown sugar, and remaining fish sauce, stirring to dissolve the sugar if necessary.

Cut the beef into thin strips and place in a bowl with the dressing and tomatoes. Toss well. Arrange the lettuce on a serving platter and pile the beef salad on top.

Serves 4

Fresh salmon patties with mango salsa

1 garlic clove, peeled
1 lb. fresh salmon, skin removed,
  roughly chopped
1 red onion, diced
1/2 cup dry breadcrumbs
1 egg
1 cup chopped cilantro
1 mango, diced
1/4 cup lime juice

Place the garlic, salmon, and half the onion in a food processor and process until coarsely minced. Add the breadcrumbs, egg, and half the cilantro and season. Mix together well and divide into six equal portions. Shape into patties, place on a plate, cover, and refrigerate for 30 minutes. To make the salsa, place the mango, 2 tablespoons lime juice, and the remaining onion and cilantro in a bowl and mix together well.

Heat a lightly greased, nonstick frying pan, add the remaining lime juice, and cook the patties for 4–5 minutes each side. They should be moist and slightly pink inside. To serve, place the patties on six serving plates and spoon the salsa on top.

Serves 6

Note: The patties can be served between foccacia with salad greens, or with a salad and bread on the side. If unavailable, fresh salmon can be replaced by canned salmon.

Mediterranean layered loaf

2 eggplants
4 zucchini
2 lbs. orange sweet potatoes
2 large red peppers
1/3 cup olive oil
9-in.-round loaf of multigrain bread
5 1/2-oz. jar pesto
3/4 cup ricotta cheese
1/3 cup grated Parmesan cheese

Cut the eggplants and zucchini into 1/2-in. slices lengthwise. Sprinkle the eggplants with salt and drain for 30 minutes, then rinse and pat dry.

Cut the sweet potatoes into 1/4-in. slices. Quarter the peppers and remove the seeds and membranes. Broil, skin-side up, until the skins have blackened. Allow to cool in a plastic bag, then remove the skins. Brush the vegetables with olive oil and broil, in batches, until lightly browned.

Cut a lid from the top of the loaf. Remove the bread from inside, leaving a 1/2-in. shell. Brush the inside of the loaf and lid with pesto. Layer the zucchini and peppers inside the loaf, then spread with the combined ricotta and Parmesan. Layer in the sweet potatoes and eggplants, pressing down to fit. Replace the lid.

Cover the loaf with plastic wrap and place on a cookie sheet. Place another cookie sheet on top and put heavy cans of food on top. Chill overnight.

Preheat the oven to 500°F. Remove the plastic wrap, return the loaf to the cookie sheet, and bake for about 10 minutes or until crispy. Cut into wedges to serve.

Serves 6

Salami pasta salad

1 red pepper
1 green pepper
4 celery stalks
1 fennel bulb, trimmed
1 red onion
6 oz. pepper-coated salami, thickly
  sliced
½ cup chopped Italian parsley
12 oz. mixed colored fettucine,
  broken into short pieces

Dressing
½ cup olive oil
3 tablespoons lemon juice
2½ tablespoons Dijon mustard
1 teaspoon sugar
1 garlic clove, crushed

Slice the red and green peppers into strips and place them in a large bowl. Slice the celery and add to the bowl. Cut the fennel and onion in half, then slice and add to the bowl. Cut the salami into strips and add to the bowl along with the parsley.

Cook the fettucine in a large saucepan of rapidly boiling, salted water until just tender. Drain and rinse in cold water. Transfer the cooked pasta to the bowl and mix thoroughly with the peppers, celery, fennel, onion, parsley, and salami.

To make the dressing, combine the olive oil, lemon juice, mustard, sugar, and crushed garlic and season to taste with salt and plenty of cracked pepper. Pour over the salad and toss well to coat.

Serves 8

Shrimp skewers with coconut sambal

1/3 cup coconut cream
1/4 cup lime juice
2 tablespoons soy sauce
1 tablespoon grated lime zest
2 teaspoons chopped red chili
1 teaspoon brown sugar
1/2 teaspoon shrimp paste
4 garlic cloves, crushed
32 medium shrimp, peeled and
  deveined, with tails intact
2 teaspoons vegetable oil
1 tablespoon chopped cilantro

mango chutney

Coconut sambal
1/4 cup unsweetened flaked or
  shredded coconut
1/4 cup sesame seeds
1/2 teaspoon dried garlic flakes
1/4 teaspoon ground coriander
1/4 teaspoon ground cumin
1/4 cup roasted unsalted peanuts,
  roughly chopped

Soak eight bamboo skewers in water for 30 minutes.

Combine the coconut cream, lime juice, soy sauce, lime zest, chili, sugar, shrimp paste, and garlic and mix until the sugar dissolves.

Thread four shrimp on each skewer. Place on a nonmetallic plate and pour the marinade over them and refrigerate, covered, for 1 hour.

To make the sambal, toast the coconut in a dry frying pan for 1–2 minutes or until golden, then add the sesame seeds, garlic flakes, spices, and 1/2 teaspoon salt and cook for about 30 seconds. Remove from the heat and stir in the peanuts. Spoon into a small serving bowl.

Heat a ridged, cast-iron grill pan or barbecue to high and brush with a little oil. Cook the shrimp on both sides for 2–3 minutes or until pink and cooked. Place on a platter and sprinkle with cilantro. Serve with the sambal and chutney.

Serves 4

Roast beef and spinach salad with horseradish

1/2 lb. green beans, trimmed
1-lb. top round beefsteak, cut into
   1 1/4-in.-thick pieces
1 red onion, peeled and halved
1 tablespoon olive oil
2 1/4 cups baby spinach
1 1/2 cups watercress leaves
1 1/3 cups sun-dried tomatoes
1/2 cup plain yogurt
1 tablespoon creamed horseradish
2 tablespoons lemon juice
2 tablespoons whipping cream
2 garlic cloves
2–3 dashes hot pepper sauce

sea salt to taste

Bring a saucepan of water to a boil, add the beans, and cook for 4 minutes or until tender. Drain, then rinse under cold water. When cool, drain and set aside. Preheat a broiler or barbecue. Brush the steak and onion with oil and cook the steak for 2 minutes each side or until rare. Remove the steak and leave for 5 minutes. Meanwhile, cook the onion for 2–3 minutes each side or until charred.

Place the spinach, watercress, tomatoes, and beans in a large salad bowl. In a small bowl, whisk together the yogurt, horseradish, lemon juice, whipping cream, garlic, hot pepper sauce, and some black pepper to taste. Chill for 15 minutes.

Slice the beef thinly across the grain and layer carefully over the salad. Slice the cooked onion, add to the salad, and drizzle with the dressing. Season well with sea salt and freshly ground black pepper.

Serves 4

Note: This cooking time will result in rare beef. Cook for a little longer if you prefer your beef medium or well done.

Caesar salad

3 eggs
3 garlic cloves, crushed
2–3 anchovy fillets
1 teaspoon Worcestershire sauce
2 tablespoons lime juice
1 teaspoon Dijon mustard
3/4 cup olive oil
3 slices white bread
1 tablespoon butter
1 tablespoon olive oil, extra
3 slices bacon
1 large head romaine lettuce
3/4 cup shaved Parmesan cheese

Process the eggs, garlic, anchovies, Worcestershire sauce, lime juice, and mustard in a food processor until smooth. With the motor running, add the oil in a thin, continuous stream to produce a creamy dressing. Season to taste with salt and freshly ground black pepper.

Cut the crusts off the bread, then cut the bread into 1/2-in. cubes. Heat the butter and extra olive oil in a frying pan over medium heat, add the bread, and cook for 5–8 minutes or until crisp, then remove from the pan. Cook the bacon in the same pan for 3 minutes or until it is crispy, then break into bite-sized pieces.

Toss the lettuce leaves with the dressing, then stir in the croutons and bacon and top with Parmesan.

Serves 4–6

Tequila and lime grilled shrimp

32 large shrimp
1/2 cup lime juice
1/4 cup tequila
2 small red chilies, finely chopped
3 tablespoons chopped cilantro
2 tablespoons olive oil
2 garlic cloves, crushed

Green tomato salsa
1 green tomato, seeded and diced
2 tablespoons finely chopped red
    onion
2 green chilies, seeded and finely
    diced
1/2 cup chopped cilantro
1 garlic clove, chopped
1 tablespoon olive oil

1 avocado
1 tablespoon lime juice

Soak eight wooden skewers in cold water for 30 minutes. Peel and devein the shrimp, leaving the tails intact. Thread four shrimp onto each skewer. Lay out the skewers in a single layer in a nonmetallic dish.

Combine the lime juice, tequila, chilies, cilantro, oil, and garlic in a small bowl, then pour over the shrimp. Cover and marinate in the refrigerator for 30 minutes.

To make the salsa, mix together the diced tomato, onion, chilies, cilantro, garlic, and olive oil, then season. Cover and refrigerate until needed.

Cook the skewers on a hot, lightly oiled, ridged, cast-iron grill pan or barbecue for 3–5 minutes or until pink and cooked through, brushing with the marinade during cooking to keep the shrimp moist.

Before serving, halve the avocado, remove the pit, dice the flesh into 1/2-in. pieces, then gently mix the avocado into the salsa, stirring in the lime juice at the same time. Season to taste, then serve with the shrimp.

Serves 4

Lamb, bell pepper, and cucumber salad

1 red onion, very thinly sliced
1 red pepper, very thinly sliced
1 green pepper, very thinly sliced
2 small cucumbers, cut into strips
1/3 cup shredded mint
3 tablespoons chopped dill
1/4 cup olive oil
1 1/3 lbs. lamb fillets
1/3 cup lemon juice
2 small garlic cloves, crushed
1/2 cup extra-virgin olive oil

Combine the onion, red and green peppers, cucumber, mint, and dill in a large bowl.

Heat a ridged, cast-iron grill pan or frying pan until hot. Drizzle with the oil and cook the lamb for 2–3 minutes on each side or until it is tender but still a little pink. Remove from the pan and allow to cool for 5 minutes. Thinly slice the lamb and add to the salad, tossing to mix.

Combine the lemon juice and garlic in a small bowl, then whisk in the extra-virgin olive oil with a fork until well combined. Season with salt and black pepper, then toss the dressing gently through the salad.

Serves 4

Note: This salad is delicious served on fresh or toasted Turkish bread spread with hummus.

Brown rice and puy lentils with pine nuts and spinach

1 cup brown rice
1/2 cup extra-virgin olive oil
1 red onion, diced
2 garlic cloves, crushed
1 carrot, diced
2 celery stalks, diced
1 cup puy lentils (see Note)
2 tomatoes, seeded and diced
3 tablespoons chopped cilantro
3 tablespoons chopped mint
2 tablespoons balsamic vinegar
1 tablespoon lemon juice
2 tablespoons toasted pine nuts
2 cups baby spinach leaves, washed

Bring a large saucepan of water to a boil. Add 1 teaspoon salt and the rice and cook for 20 minutes or until tender. Drain and rinse under cold running water.

Heat 2 tablespoons oil in a saucepan and add the onion, garlic, carrot, and celery. Cook over low heat for 5 minutes or until softened, then add the puy lentils and 1 1/2 cups water. Bring to a boil and simmer for 15 minutes or until tender. Drain well, but do not rinse. Combine with the rice, tomatoes, cilantro, and mint in a large bowl.

Whisk the remaining oil with the balsamic vinegar and lemon juice, then season well with salt and freshly ground black pepper. Pour over the salad, add the pine nuts and spinach, and toss well to combine.

Serves 6–8

Note: Puy lentils are green French lentils available at specialty food stores. You can substitute green or brown lentils.

Risoni and broccoli salad with fresh herb dressing

8 garlic cloves, unpeeled
2 tablespoons extra-virgin olive oil
1/2 cup mayonnaise
1/2 cup crème fraîche
1/3 cup pesto
2 tablespoons lemon juice
1 cup broccoli florets
1 1/2 cups risoni (rice-shaped pasta)
1/3 cup toasted slivered almonds
1 tablespoon finely chopped parsley
1 tablespoon finely chopped chives

shaved Parmesan cheese

Preheat the oven to 350°F. Toss the garlic cloves in the olive oil and bake for 45 minutes or until they are soft and golden.

Squeeze two of the garlic cloves from their skins and place in a food processor. Add the mayonnaise, crème fraîche, pesto, and lemon juice and process until just combined, then set aside until needed.

Meanwhile, steam the broccoli florets for a few minutes, then rinse under cold water and drain well. Bring a large saucepan of water to a boil, then add 1 teaspoon of salt and the risoni and cook for 8–10 minutes or until al dente. Drain.

Add the almonds, dressing, parsley, and chives to the risoni while still warm and toss with the broccoli in a large bowl. Serve in deep salad bowls garnished with shaved Parmesan and a roasted garlic clove on each portion.

Serves 6

Variation: Adding some cooked, peeled jumbo shrimp will give the salad a special touch.

Beef satay salad

2 teaspoons tamarind pulp
1/2 teaspoon sesame oil
2 tablespoons soy sauce
2 teaspoons brown sugar
2 garlic cloves, crushed
1 tablespoon lime juice
1 1/2 lbs. rump steak
1 tablespoon peanut oil
6 large romaine lettuce leaves,
    washed, dried, and shredded
1 red pepper, julienned
2 cups bean sprouts
2 tablespoons fried onion flakes

Satay sauce
2 red chilies, chopped
1/2 teaspoon shrimp paste
1 garlic clove
6 red Asian shallots
2 teaspoons peanut oil
1 cup coconut milk
1 tablespoon lime juice
3/4 cup unsalted roasted peanuts,
    finely ground in a food processor
1 tablespoon kecap manis
1 tablespoon brown sugar
1 tablespoon fish sauce
2 kaffir lime leaves, shredded

Combine the tamarind pulp and
1/4 cup of boiling water and allow
to cool. Mash the pulp with your
fingertips to dissolve it, then strain,
reserving the liquid. Discard the pulp.

Put the sesame oil, soy sauce, sugar,
garlic, lime juice, and 2 tablespoons
of tamarind water in a large bowl. Add
the steak, turn to coat, and cover with
plastic wrap. Chill for 2 hours.

Meanwhile, to make the satay sauce,
process the chilies, shrimp paste,
garlic, and shallots to a paste in a
food processor. Heat the oil in a frying
pan and cook the paste for 3 minutes.
Add the coconut milk, lime juice,
ground peanuts, remaining tamarind
water, kecap manis, sugar, fish sauce,
and kaffir lime leaves. Cook over
medium heat until thickened. Thin
with 1/2 cup water and return to a boil
for 2 minutes. Season to taste.

Heat the peanut oil in a frying pan
over high heat and cook the steak
for 3 minutes on each side or until
medium-rare. Leave for 3 minutes,
then slice thinly. Toss the steak slices
in a large bowl with the lettuce, red
pepper, and bean sprouts. Pile onto
serving plates, drizzle with the satay
sauce, and sprinkle with the fried
onion flakes.

Serves 4

Crab salad with green mango and coconut

2 garlic cloves, peeled
2 small red chilies
2 tablespoons dried shrimp
2 tablespoons fish sauce
3 tablespoons lime juice
3 teaspoons brown sugar
1/2 cup shredded coconut (see Notes)
1 1/2 cups shredded green mango
1/2 cup mint leaves (torn if very big)
1/2 cup cilantro
3 kaffir lime leaves, shredded
2 teaspoons thinly shredded, pickled
  ginger
1 lb. fresh crabmeat

banana leaves (optional)
crushed, toasted peanuts
lime wedges

Preheat the oven to 350°F. Place the garlic, chilies, dried shrimp, and 1/2 teaspoon salt in a mortar and pestle. Pound to a paste, then whisk in the fish sauce, lime juice, and brown sugar with a fork.

Place the shredded coconut on a baking tray and bake for 3–5 minutes, shaking the tray occasionally to ensure even toasting. Watch the coconut closely, as it will burn easily.

Place the shredded mango in a large bowl and add the mint, cilantro, kaffir lime leaves, ginger, coconut, and crabmeat. Pour on the dressing and toss together gently.

Place a piece of banana leaf (if using) in each serving bowl. Mound some crab salad on top, sprinkle with the peanuts, and serve immediately with lime wedges.

Serves 4–6

Notes: Freshly shredded coconut is delicious, so if you have the time, remove the skin from a coconut and shred using a vegetable peeler. The banana leaves are for presentation only and are not edible.

Spicy lamb and noodle salad

1 tablespoon five-spice powder
1/4 cup vegetable oil
2 garlic cloves, crushed
2 lamb fillets (about 1/2 lb. each)
16 oz. fresh Shanghai (wheat) noodles
1 1/2 teaspoons sesame oil
1/3 cup snow pea sprouts
1/2 red pepper, thinly sliced
4 scallions, thinly sliced diagonally
2 tablespoons sesame seeds, toasted

Dressing
1 tablespoon finely chopped fresh
  ginger
1 tablespoon Chinese black vinegar
1 tablespoon Chinese rice wine
2 tablespoons peanut oil
2 teaspoons chili oil

Combine the five-spice powder, 2 tablespoons of the vegetable oil, and garlic in a large bowl. Add the lamb and turn to coat well. Cover and marinate for 30 minutes.

Cook the noodles in a large saucepan of boiling water for 4–5 minutes or until tender. Drain, rinse with cold water, and drain again. Add the sesame oil and toss to combine.

Heat the remaining vegetable oil in a large frying pan. Cook the lamb over medium-high heat for 3 minutes each side for medium-rare, or until cooked to your liking. Cool for 5 minutes, then slice thinly across the grain.

To make the dressing, combine the ginger, Chinese black vinegar, rice wine, peanut oil, and chili oil.

Place the noodles, lamb strips, snow pea sprouts, red pepper, scallions, and the dressing in a large bowl and toss gently until well combined. Sprinkle with the sesame seeds and serve immediately.

Serves 4

Crab, Camembert, and fusilli frittata

1 cup tricolored fusilli
1 tablespoon olive oil
1 very small red onion, finely chopped
1 large Roma (plum) tomato, roughly chopped
1/3 cup semidry (sun-blushed) tomatoes, roughly chopped
2 tablespoons finely chopped cilantro
2/3 cup fresh-cooked or canned crabmeat
5 oz. Camembert cheese, rind removed, cut into small pieces
6 eggs plus 2 egg yolks

Cook the pasta in a large saucepan of boiling water until al dente. Drain, rinse, then drain again and set aside to cool. Meanwhile, heat half the oil in a small frying pan over low heat, add the onion, and cook for 4–5 minutes or until softened but not browned. Transfer to a bowl and add the Roma tomato, semidry tomatoes, and cilantro. Squeeze out any excess moisture from the crabmeat and add the meat to the bowl. Add half the cheese to the bowl, then add the cooled pasta. Mix well. Beat together the six eggs and the two extra yolks, then stir into the tomato and crab mixture. Season to taste.

Heat the remaining oil in the frying pan, pour in the frittata mixture, and cook over low heat for 25 minutes. Preheat the broiler to low. Sprinkle the remaining Camembert over the frittata before placing it under the broiler for 10–15 minutes or until cooked and golden brown on top. Remove from the broiler and leave for 5 minutes. Cut into slices and serve with salad and some bread.

Serves 4–6

Asian tofu salad

1 large red pepper
1 large green pepper
2 cups bean sprouts
4 scallions, sliced diagonally
1/4 cup chopped cilantro
3 cups shredded Chinese cabbage
1/4 cup chopped roasted peanuts
16 oz. firm tofu
1/4 cup peanut oil

Dressing
2 tablespoons sweet chili sauce
2 tablespoons lime juice
1/2 teaspoon sesame oil
1 1/2 tablespoons light soy sauce
1 garlic clove, finely chopped
3 teaspoons finely grated fresh ginger
1/4 cup peanut oil

Thinly slice the peppers and combine with the bean sprouts, scallions, cilantro, cabbage, and peanuts.

Drain the liquid from the tofu and cut into 4 x 1 in. slices. Heat the oil in a large frying pan. Cook the tofu for 2–3 minutes on each side or until it is golden with a crispy edge, and add to the salad.

To make the dressing, mix together the chili sauce, lime juice, oil, soy, garlic, and ginger. Whisk in the peanut oil, then toss through the salad and serve immediately.

Serves 4–6

Shrimp and rice noodle salad

8 oz. rice stick noodles
1 1/2 lbs. medium cooked shrimp, peeled and deveined, with tails intact
1 carrot, coarsely grated
1 small cucumber, thinly sliced
1 cup cilantro
1/2 cup roasted unsalted peanuts, chopped
1/4 cup crisp fried shallots (see Note)

Dressing
1/2 cup rice vinegar
1 tablespoon brown sugar
1 garlic clove, finely chopped
2 red chilies, finely chopped
1/4 cup fish sauce
1/4 cup lime juice
2 tablespoons peanut oil

Soak the noodles in boiling water in a large, heatproof bowl for 10 minutes. Drain, rinse under cold water to cool, and drain again. Place in a large serving bowl.

Add the shrimp, carrot, cucumber, and cilantro to the bowl and toss.

To make the dressing, combine the vinegar, sugar, and garlic in a small saucepan and bring to a boil, then reduce the heat and simmer for 3 minutes to slightly reduce the liquid. Transfer to a bowl and add the chili, fish sauce, and lime juice. Slowly whisk in the oil and season to taste.

Toss the dressing through the salad, then sprinkle with the peanuts and crisp fried shallots and serve.

Serves 4

Note: Crisp fried shallots are red Asian shallot flakes used as a garnish in Southeast Asia. They are available from Asian markets.

Chargrilled vegetable terrine

8 large slices chargrilled eggplant,
    drained
10 slices chargrilled red pepper,
    drained
8 slices chargrilled zucchini, drained
1 1/2 cups ricotta cheese
2 garlic cloves, crushed
1/4 cup arugula
3 marinated artichokes, drained and
    sliced
1/2 cup semidry (sun-blushed)
    tomatoes, drained and chopped
1/2 cup marinated mushrooms,
    drained and halved

Line a 9 x 5 x 3 in. loaf pan with plastic wrap, leaving a generous overhang on each side. Line the base with half the eggplant, cutting to fit. Then layer in half the pepper, then all of the zucchini.

Beat the ricotta and garlic together until smooth. Season, then spread evenly over the zucchini. Press down firmly and top with the arugula leaves. Arrange the marinated artichoke, tomato, and mushrooms in three strips over the arugula.

Top with another layer of pepper and finish with the eggplant. Cover securely with the overhanging plastic wrap. Top with a piece of cardboard and weigh it down. Chill overnight.

Peel back the plastic wrap and carefully turn out the terrine onto a plate. Remove the plastic wrap and cut into thick slices to serve.

Serves 8

Wild rice and roast chicken with Asian dressing

1 cup wild rice
1 cup jasmine rice
1 Chinese barbecued roast chicken
  (see Note)
¼ cup chopped mint
¼ cup chopped cilantro
1 large cucumber
6 scallions
½ cup roasted peanuts, roughly
  chopped
⅓ cup mirin
2 tablespoons Chinese rice wine
1 tablespoon soy sauce
1 tablespoon lime juice
2 tablespoons sweet chili sauce,
  plus extra to serve

Bring a large saucepan of water to a boil and add 1 teaspoon of salt and the wild rice. Cook for 30 minutes, add the jasmine rice, and cook for another 10 minutes or until tender. Drain the rice, rinse under cold water, and drain again.

Shred the chicken (including the skin) into bite-sized pieces, place in a large bowl, and add the mint and cilantro. Cut the cucumber through the center (do not peel) and thinly slice diagonally. Slice the scallions diagonally. Add the cucumber, scallions, rice, and peanuts to the bowl with the chicken.

Mix together the mirin, rice wine, soy, lime juice, and sweet chili sauce in a small jar, pour over the salad, and toss to combine. Pile the salad onto serving plates and serve with extra chili sauce.

Serves 8

Note: It is important to use a Chinese barbecued chicken, available from Asian markets. The five-spice powder and soy sauce used to cook it will add to the flavor of the dish.

Modern salad Niçoise

¼ cup lemon juice
1 garlic clove, crushed
¾ cup olive oil
14 oz. waxy potatoes
3 eggs
1 cup green beans, trimmed
1 green pepper, seeded and sliced
½ cup black olives
1 ½ cups firm, ripe tomatoes, cut into
  wedges
½ cup cucumber, cut into chunks
3 scallions, cut into 1-in. pieces
1 ½ lbs. fresh tuna steaks

Place the lemon juice, garlic, and ½ cup olive oil in a jar with a screw-top lid. Season to taste and shake the jar well to combine.

Boil the potatoes in a saucepan of salted water for 10–12 minutes or until tender. Add the eggs for the final 8 minutes of cooking. Drain, cool the eggs under cold water, then peel and quarter. Cool the potatoes, then cut into chunks. Bring a saucepan of salted water to a boil, add the green beans, and blanch for 3 minutes. Drain and rinse under cold water. Drain well, then slice in half diagonally.

Place the potato and beans in a large bowl and add the pepper, olives, tomatoes, cucumber, and scallions. Strain the garlic from the dressing, then shake again so it is combined. Pour half over the salad, toss, and transfer to a serving dish.

Heat a frying pan over very high heat. Add the remaining olive oil and allow to heat. Season the tuna steaks well on both sides and cook for 2 minutes on each side or until rare. Allow the tuna to cool for 5 minutes, then slice thinly. Arrange on top of the salad with the eggs and drizzle with the remaining dressing.

Serves 4

Asian pork salad

2 teaspoons rice vinegar
1 small red chili, finely chopped
2 tablespoons light soy sauce
1 teaspoon julienned fresh ginger
1/4 teaspoon sesame oil
1 star anise
2 teaspoons lime juice
9 oz. Chinese roasted pork (char siu)
1 cup snow pea sprouts
2 scallions, thinly sliced diagonally
1/2 red pepper, thinly sliced

For the dressing, combine the vinegar, chili, soy sauce, ginger, sesame oil, star anise, and lime juice in a small saucepan. Gently warm for 2 minutes or until it is just about to boil, then set aside to cool. Once it is cool, remove the star anise.

Thinly slice the pork and place in a serving bowl. Pick over the sprouts, discarding any brown or broken ones, and add to the pork. Add the scallion and pepper, pour on the dressing, and toss well.

Serves 4

Shrimp and bean salad

1 cup dried cannellini beans
2 red peppers, cut into large, flat
  pieces
1 1/2 cups green beans, trimmed
1/2 loaf day-old ciabatta bread or other
  crusty loaf
1/3 cup olive oil
1 large garlic clove, finely chopped
2 lbs. raw medium shrimp, peeled
  and deveined, with tails intact
1 1/2 cups Italian parsley

Dressing
1/4 cup lemon juice
1/4 cup olive oil
2 tablespoons capers, rinsed,
  drained, and chopped
1 teaspoon sugar (optional)

Soak the cannellini beans in a large bowl of cold water for 8 hours. Drain, then rinse the beans well, transfer to a saucepan, cover with cold water, and cook for 20–30 minutes or until tender. Drain, rinse under cold water, drain again, and put in a serving bowl.

Cook the pepper, skin-side up, under a hot broiler until the skin blackens and blisters. Cool in a plastic bag, then peel. Cut into strips and add to the bowl.

Cook the green beans in a saucepan of boiling water for 3–4 minutes or until tender. Drain and add to the serving bowl. Cut the bread into six slices, then cut each slice in four. Heat 1/4 cup of the oil in a frying pan and cook the bread over medium heat on each side until golden. Remove from the pan.

Heat the remaining oil in the frying pan, add the garlic and shrimp, and cook for 1–2 minutes or until the shrimp are pink and cooked. Add to the salad with the parsley.

Combine the dressing ingredients, then season. Toss the dressing and bread through the salad.

Serves 4

Marinated grilled tofu salad with ginger miso dressing

1/3 cup tamari, shoyu, or light soy sauce
2 teaspoons vegetable oil
2 garlic cloves, crushed
1 teaspoon grated fresh ginger
1 teaspoon chili paste
16 oz. firm tofu, cut into 1-in. cubes
4 cups mixed lettuce leaves
1 cucumber, finely sliced
1 1/2 cups cherry tomatoes, halved
2 teaspoons vegetable oil, extra

Dressing
2 teaspoons white miso paste
2 tablespoons mirin
1 teaspoon sesame oil
1 teaspoon grated fresh ginger
1 teaspoon finely chopped chives
1 tablespoon toasted sesame seeds

Mix together the tamari, oil, garlic, ginger, chili paste, and 1/2 teaspoon salt in a bowl. Add the tofu and mix until well coated. Marinate for at least 10 minutes, or preferably overnight. Drain and reserve the marinade.

To make the dressing, combine the miso with 1/2 cup hot water and leave until the miso dissolves. Add the mirin, sesame oil, ginger, chives, and sesame seeds and stir thoroughly until it begins to thicken.

Combine the mixed lettuce leaves, cucumber, and tomato in a serving bowl and leave until ready to serve.

Heat the extra oil in a frying pan. Add the tofu and cook over medium heat for 4 minutes or until golden brown. Pour on the reserved marinade and cook for 1 minute over high heat. Remove from the pan and allow to cool for 5 minutes.

Add the tofu to the salad, drizzle with the dressing, and toss well.

Serves 4

Note: Miso is Japanese bean paste and plays an important part in their cuisine. It is commonly used in soups, dressings, on grilled foods, and as a flavoring for pickles.

Chicken and tzatziki wrap

½ cucumber, seeded and grated
½ cup low-fat natural yogurt
¼ teaspoon lemon juice
1 tablespoon chopped mint
4 skinless chicken thigh fillets
pinch paprika
4 sheets lavash or other flatbread
  (see Note)
4 large Bibb lettuce leaves

Sprinkle the grated cucumber with ½ teaspoon salt. Leave the cucumber for 10 minutes, then drain and mix with the yogurt, lemon juice, and mint. Season to taste.

Flatten the chicken thigh fillets with a meat mallet or rolling pin, season, and sprinkle with the paprika. Grill the fillets for 5–7 minutes on each side or until cooked through.

Lay out the lavash breads and place a large Bibb lettuce leaf on each. Spread each with one quarter of the tzatziki, then top with a sliced chicken fillet. Roll up, folding one end closed. Wrap in baking parchment to serve.

Makes 4

Note: If you can't find lavash, use any other flatbread that will roll up easily, such as a tortilla.

Pepper-crusted salmon salad

1 tablespoon coarsely ground black
  pepper
4 salmon fillets (approximately
  6 oz. each), skin removed
1/3 cup mayonnaise
1 1/2 tablespoons lemon juice
2 teaspoons creamed horseradish
1 small garlic clove, crushed
2 tablespoons chopped parsley
1 cup watercress
3 tablespoons olive oil
2 tablespoons butter
1 cup Bibb lettuce

Mix the pepper and 1/4 teaspoon salt together in a bowl and coat both sides of each salmon fillet, pressing the pepper down firmly with your fingers. Chill for 30 minutes.

Blend the mayonnaise, lemon juice, horseradish, garlic, parsley, half of the watercress, 1 tablespoon of oil, and 1 tablespoon of warm water in a food processor for 1 minute. Chill.

Heat the butter and 1 tablespoon oil in a large frying pan until bubbling. Add the salmon fillets and cook over medium-high heat for 2–3 minutes each side or until cooked to your liking. Remove from the pan and allow to cool slightly.

Wash and dry the Bibb lettuce and tear into small pieces. Arrange the lettuce and remaining watercress in the center of four serving plates and drizzle lightly with the remaining olive oil. Break each salmon fillet into four or five pieces and arrange over the lettuce. Pour the dressing over the salmon and in a circle around the outside of the leaves.

Serves 4

Roasted tomato and pasta salad with pesto

½ cup olive oil
2 cups cherry tomatoes
5 garlic cloves, unpeeled
2 cups penne pasta
⅓ cup pesto
3 tablespoons balsamic vinegar

basil leaves

Preheat the oven to 350°F. Place 2 tablespoons of oil in a roasting dish and place in the hot oven for 5 minutes. Add the tomatoes and garlic to the dish, season well, and toss until the tomatoes are well coated. Return to the oven and roast for 30 minutes.

Meanwhile, cook the pasta in a large saucepan of rapidly boiling water until al dente. Drain and transfer to a large serving bowl.

Squeeze the flesh from the roasted garlic cloves into a bowl. Add the remaining olive oil, the pesto, vinegar, and 3 tablespoons of the tomato cooking juices. Season with a little salt and pepper and toss to combine. Add to the pasta and mix well, ensuring that the pasta is coated in the dressing. Gently stir in the cherry tomatoes, then sprinkle with basil. This salad can be prepared up to 4 hours ahead and served warm or cold.

Serves 4

Beef teriyaki with cucumber salad

1/3 cup soy sauce
2 tablespoons mirin
1 tablespoon sake (optional)
1 garlic clove, crushed
1 teaspoon grated fresh ginger
4 filets mignons
1 teaspoon sugar
1 teaspoon toasted sesame seeds

Cucumber salad
1 large cucumber, peeled, seeded, and diced
1/2 red pepper, diced
2 scallions, thinly sliced diagonally
2 teaspoons sugar
1 tablespoon rice wine vinegar

Combine the soy, mirin, sake, garlic, and ginger and pour over the steaks. Cover with plastic wrap and chill for at least 30 minutes.

To make the cucumber salad, place the cucumber, pepper, and scallions in a bowl. Place the sugar, rice wine vinegar, and 1/4 cup water in a saucepan and stir over medium heat until the sugar dissolves. Increase the heat and simmer for 3–4 minutes or until thickened. Pour over the cucumber salad, stir to combine, and leave to cool completely.

Spray a nonstick pan with oil and heat until very hot. Drain the steaks and reserve the marinade. Cook for 3–4 minutes on each side or until cooked to your liking. Allow the meat to cool for 5–10 minutes.

Place the sugar and the reserved marinade in a saucepan and heat, stirring, until the sugar has dissolved. Bring to a boil and simmer for 2 minutes. Keep warm.

Slice each steak into 1/2-in. strips and arrange a steak on each plate. Spoon on some of the marinade, some salad, and garnish with sesame seeds. Serve with steamed rice and the remaining cucumber salad.

Serves 4

Tofu kabobs with cilantro miso

1 large red pepper, cut into squares
12 button mushrooms, halved
6 pickling onions, quartered
3 zucchini, cut into 1½-in. chunks
16 oz. firm tofu, cut into 1-in. cubes
½ cup light olive oil
¼ cup light soy sauce
2 garlic cloves, crushed
2 teaspoons grated fresh ginger

Cilantro miso
½ cup unsalted roasted peanuts
2 cups firmly packed cilantro
2 tablespoons white miso paste
2 garlic cloves
½ cup olive oil

Soak twelve wooden skewers in cold water for 10 minutes. Thread the vegetable pieces and tofu alternately onto the skewers, then place in a large, rectangular baking dish.

Combine the olive oil, soy sauce, garlic, and ginger in a bowl, then pour half the mixture over the kabobs. Cover with plastic wrap and marinate for 1 hour.

To make the cilantro miso, finely chop the peanuts, cilantro, miso paste, and garlic in a food processor. Slowly add the olive oil while the machine is still running and blend to a smooth paste.

Heat a large frying pan and cook the kabobs, turning and brushing frequently with the remaining marinade, for 4–6 minutes or until the edges are slightly brown. Serve with steamed rice and a little of the cilantro miso.

Serves 4

very good - not enough for 4 -

Chili chicken and cashew salad

3 tablespoons sweet chili sauce
2 tablespoons lime juice
2 teaspoons fish sauce
2 tablespoons chopped cilantro
1 garlic clove, crushed
1 small red chili, finely chopped
1 1/2 teaspoons grated fresh ginger
2 tablespoons olive oil
1 1/3 lbs. boneless, skinless chicken breasts
1 cup salad leaves
1 cup cherry tomatoes, halved
1/2 cup cucumber, cut into bite-sized chunks
1/2 cup snow pea sprouts, trimmed
1/2 cup cashew nuts, roughly chopped

Combine the chili sauce, lime juice, fish sauce, cilantro, garlic, chili, ginger, and 1 tablespoon of the oil in a large bowl.

Heat the remaining oil in a frying pan over medium heat until hot and cook the chicken for 5–8 minutes on each side or until cooked through. While still hot, slice each breast into 1/2-in. slices and toss in the bowl with the dressing. Leave to cool slightly.

Combine the salad leaves, cherry tomatoes, cucumber chunks, and snow pea sprouts in a serving bowl. Add the chicken and all of the dressing and toss gently until the leaves are lightly coated. Sprinkle with chopped cashews and serve.

Serves 4 *2.*

Calamari salad with salsa verde

1³/₄ lbs. small or medium calamari, cleaned, scored, and sliced into 2-in. diamonds
2 tablespoons olive oil
2 tablespoons lime juice
1 cup green beans
1 cup asparagus spears
1 teaspoon olive oil, extra
1 cup arugula

Salsa verde
1 slice white bread, crust removed
¹/₂ cup olive oil
3 tablespoons finely chopped parsley
2 teaspoons finely grated lemon zest
¹/₄ cup lemon juice
2 anchovies, finely chopped
2 tablespoons capers, rinsed and drained
1 garlic clove, crushed

Combine the calamari pieces in a bowl with the olive oil, lime juice, and a little salt and pepper, then cover with plastic wrap and place in the refrigerator to marinate for 2 hours.

To make the salsa verde, break the bread into chunks and drizzle with 2 tablespoons of oil, mixing with your hands so that the oil is absorbed. Place the bread and remaining oil in a food processor with the remaining salsa ingredients and blend to a paste. If it is too thick, thin with lemon juice and olive oil to taste.

Trim the green beans and asparagus and cut in half diagonally. Blanch the beans for 3 minutes, rinse under cold water, then drain. Blanch the asparagus for 1–2 minutes, rinse in cold water, then drain.

Heat the extra oil in a frying pan over high heat and cook the marinated calamari in batches for 3 minutes per batch or until cooked. Cool slightly.

Combine the green beans, calamari, asparagus, and arugula. Add 3 tablespoons of the salsa verde and toss gently. Arrange on a serving plate and drizzle with another tablespoon of salsa verde.

Serves 4

Spicy shrimp

2 lbs. raw jumbo shrimp
4 long red chilies, seeded
3/4 cup white wine vinegar
2 large garlic cloves, chopped
6–8 small red chilies, chopped
1/2 cup olive oil
2 cups mixed lettuce leaves

Remove the heads from the shrimp. Slice them down the back without cutting right through, leaving the tails intact. Open the shrimp out and remove the vein. Place the shrimp in a nonmetallic bowl, cover, and refrigerate until needed.

Place the long chilies in a saucepan with the vinegar and simmer over medium-high heat for 5 minutes or until the chilies are soft. Cool slightly. Transfer the chilies and 1/4 cup of the vinegar to a food processor (reserve the rest of the vinegar), then add the garlic and chopped chilies and blend until smooth.

With the motor running, gradually add the oil and remaining vinegar and process until well combined. Coat the shrimp in the sauce, then cover and chill for 30 minutes.

Heat a frying pan to high. Oil the pan, then cook the shrimp, basting with the marinade, for 2–3 minutes each side or until cooked. Boil the remaining marinade in a small saucepan, then reduce the heat and simmer for 3–4 minutes or until slightly thickened and reduced. Divide the lettuce among four plates and arrange the shrimp on top. Serve immediately with the remaining sauce.

Serves 4

Tofu fajitas

4 tablespoons light soy sauce
2 garlic cloves, crushed
16 oz. smoked tofu, cut into
  2-in. strips
8 oz. canned tomatoes
1 small onion, roughly chopped
1 small red chili, seeded and finely
  chopped
3 tablespoons chopped cilantro
1 large, ripe avocado
2 teaspoons lemon juice
1 cup sour cream
2 tablespoons vegetable oil
1 red pepper, seeded and sliced
1 yellow pepper, seeded and sliced
8 scallions, cut into 2-in. lengths
8 flour tortillas (6-in. diameter)

Place the soy sauce, garlic, and
1 teaspoon pepper in a shallow dish.
Add the tofu and toss together well.
Cover and leave to marinate.

Combine the tomatoes, onion, chili,
and cilantro in a food processor until
smooth. Season with salt and pepper.
Transfer to a small saucepan and
bring to a boil. Reduce the heat and
simmer for 10 minutes. Cool.

Halve the avocado and remove the
pit. Scoop out the flesh and add the
lemon juice and 2 tablespoons of the
sour cream. Season and mash well
with a fork.

Heat 1 tablespoon oil in a frying pan.
Add the tofu and remaining marinade
and cook, stirring, over high heat for
4–5 minutes. Remove from the pan.
Heat the remaining oil in the pan.
Add the pepper and scallions,
season, and cook for 3–4 minutes.

Dry-fry the tortillas over high heat for
5 seconds on each side.

To serve, spread a tortilla with a little
avocado mixture, tomato salsa, and
sour cream. Top with some tofu and
vegetables, fold in one end, and roll.
Repeat with the remaining tortillas
and fillings.

Serves 4

Sesame-coated tuna with cilantro salsa

4 tuna steaks
3/4 cup sesame seeds
olive oil for stir-frying
3 cups baby arugula

Cilantro salsa
2 tomatoes, seeded and diced
1 large garlic clove, crushed
2 tablespoons finely chopped
   cilantro
2 tablespoons extra-virgin olive oil
1 tablespoon lime juice

chili jam (optional)

Cut each tuna steak into three pieces. Place the sesame seeds on a sheet of waxed paper. Roll the tuna in the sesame seeds to coat. Refrigerate for 15 minutes.

For the the salsa, place the tomatoes, garlic, cilantro, oil, and lime juice in a bowl and mix together well. Cover and refrigerate until ready to use.

Fill a heavy-bottomed frying pan to 1/2 in. with the oil and place over high heat. Add the tuna in two batches and cook for 2 minutes each side (it should be pink in the center). Remove and drain on paper towels. To serve, divide the arugula among four serving plates and arrange the tuna over the top. Spoon the salsa on the side and serve immediately. Top with a teaspoon of chili jam, if desired, and season to taste.

Serves 4

Warm minted chicken and pasta salad

½ lb. cotelli or fusilli pasta
½ cup olive oil
1 large red pepper
3 skinless, boneless chicken breasts
6 scallions, cut into ¾-in. lengths
4 garlic cloves, thinly sliced
¾ cup chopped mint leaves
⅓ cup cider vinegar
2 cups spinach leaves

Cook the pasta in a large saucepan of boiling water until al dente, drain, stir in 1 tablespoon of the oil, and set aside. Meanwhile, cut the pepper into quarters, removing the seeds and membrane. Place, skin-side up, under a hot broiler for 10 minutes or until the skin blackens and blisters. Cool in a plastic bag, then peel away the skin. Cut into thin strips. Place the chicken between two sheets of plastic wrap and press with the palm of your hand until slightly flattened.

Heat 1 tablespoon of the oil in a large frying pan, add the chicken, and cook over medium heat for 2–3 minutes each side or until light brown and cooked through. Remove from the pan and cut into ¼-in. slices.

Add another tablespoon of the oil to the pan and add the scallions, sliced garlic, and pepper and cook, stirring, for 2–3 minutes or until starting to soften. Add ½ cup of the mint, the vinegar, and the remaining oil and stir until warmed through. In a large bowl, combine the pasta, chicken, spinach, onion mixture, and remaining mint and toss well, seasoning to taste. Serve warm.

Serves 4

Pork and veal terrine

8–10 thin slices bacon
1 tablespoon olive oil
1 onion, chopped
2 garlic cloves, crushed
2 lbs. ground pork and veal
1 cup fresh breadcrumbs
1 egg, beaten
1/4 cup brandy
3 teaspoons chopped thyme
1/4 cup chopped parsley

Preheat the oven to 350°F. Lightly grease a 10 x 4 1/2 in. terrine. Line the terrine with the bacon so that it hangs over the sides.

Heat the oil in a frying pan, add the onion and garlic, and cook for 2–3 minutes or until the onion is soft. Mix the onion with the ground meat, breadcrumbs, egg, brandy, thyme, and parsley in a large bowl. Season. Fry a piece of the mixture to check the seasoning and adjust if necessary.

Spoon the mixture into the lined terrine, pressing down firmly. Fold the bacon over the top, cover it with aluminum foil, and place the terrine in a baking dish.

Place enough cold water in the baking dish to come halfway up the side of the terrine. Bake for 1–1 1/4 hours or until the juices run clear when pierced with a skewer. Remove the terrine from the baking dish and pour off the excess juices. Cover with foil, then put a piece of cardboard, cut to fit, on top of the terrine. Put cans of food on top of the cardboard to compress the terrine. Refrigerate overnight, then cut into slices to serve.

Serves 6

Roast duck salad with chili dressing

½ teaspoon chili flakes
2½ tablespoons fish sauce
1 tablespoon lime juice
2 teaspoons grated brown sugar
1 Chinese roasted duck
1 small red onion, thinly sliced
1 tablespoon julienned fresh ginger
⅓ cup roughly chopped cilantro
⅓ cup roughly chopped mint leaves
½ cup roasted cashews
small head Bibb lettuce

Place the chili flakes in a frying pan and dry-fry for 30 seconds, then grind to a powder in a mortar and pestle or spice grinder. Combine the chili with the fish sauce, lime juice, and brown sugar in a bowl and set aside.

Remove the flesh from the duck and cut it into bite-sized pieces. Place the duck in a bowl with the onion, ginger, cilantro, mint, and cashews. Pour in the dressing and toss gently.

Place the lettuce on a serving platter. Top with the duck salad and serve.

Serves 4–6

Seafood salad

1 lb. small squid
2 lbs. large clams
2 lbs. black mussels
1 lb. raw medium shrimp, peeled,
  deveined, tails intact
5 tablespoons finely chopped
  Italian parsley

Dressing
2 tablespoons lemon juice
1/3 cup olive oil
1 garlic clove, crushed

Gently pull apart the body and tentacles of the squid to separate. Remove the head by cutting below the eyes. Push out the beak and discard. Pull the quill from the body of the squid and discard. Under cold running water, pull away all the skin (the flaps can be used). Rinse well, then slice the squid into rings.

Scrub the clams and mussels and remove the beards. Discard any that are cracked or don't close when tapped. Rinse under running water. Fill a saucepan with 3/4 in. water, add the clams and mussels, cover, and boil for 4–5 minutes or until the shells open. Remove, reserving the liquid. Discard any that do not open. Remove the mussels and clams from their shells and place in a bowl.

Bring 4 cups water to a boil and add the shrimp and squid. Cook for 3–4 minutes or until the shrimp turn pink and the squid is tender. Drain and add to the clams and mussels.

To make the dressing, whisk all of the ingredients together. Season. Pour over the seafood, add 4 tablespoons of the parsley, and toss to coat. Cover and refrigerate for 30–40 minutes. Sprinkle with the remaining parsley and serve with fresh bread.

Serves 4

Penne with shrimp

3 Roma (plum) tomatoes
$3/4$ lb. penne pasta
1 lb. cooked medium shrimp
$2\,1/4$ cups spinach leaves
4 oz. goat cheese, crumbled
$1/4$ cup pine nuts, toasted

Garlic dressing
2 garlic cloves, crushed
$1/4$ cup extra-virgin olive oil
2 teaspoons finely grated lemon zest
2 tablespoons lemon juice
1 tablespoon chopped Italian parsley

Preheat the oven to 350°F. Cut each Roma tomato lengthwise into six wedges and bake on a baking sheet lined with parchment paper for 45 minutes or until the wedges are just starting to dry out around the edges. Remove and cool.

Cook the penne in a large saucepan of rapidly boiling, salted water for 12 minutes or until al dente. Drain and cool. Transfer to a large bowl.

Meanwhile, peel the shrimp, leaving the tails intact. Gently pull out the dark vein from each shrimp back, starting at the head.

Add the cooled tomatoes, shrimp, spinach, and cheese to the pasta and toss well.

For the garlic dressing, place all the ingredients in a screw-top jar, secure the lid tightly, and shake well. Pour over the salad and toss until well distributed. Sprinkle with pine nuts and serve.

Serves 4

Thai marinated octopus salad

8 baby octopus or 4 large octopus,
  cut in half (about ¾ lb.)
1 cup sweet chili sauce
2 tablespoons lime juice
1 lemongrass stalk, trimmed and
  finely chopped
2 small cucumbers
2-oz. head Bibb lettuce, torn into
  rough pieces
1 cup cilantro, with stems

Using a small knife, cut between the head and tentacles of the octopus, just below the eyes. Grasp the body of the octopus and push the beak out with your finger. Cut the eyes from the head of the octopus and discard the eye section. Carefully slit through one side, avoiding the ink sac, and scrape out the gut. Rinse under running water to remove any remaining gut.

Put the octopus in a bowl and add the chili sauce, lime juice, and lemongrass. Stir until well mixed. Cover with plastic wrap and chill for at least 4 hours.

Cut the cucumbers into 2½-in. pieces and discard the seeds. Cut them into batons.

Heat a ridged, cast-iron grill pan until hot. Remove the octopus from the marinade, reserving the marinade, and cook for 2–3 minutes or until cooked through. Cool slightly. Arrange the lettuce and cilantro around the edge of a plate and pile the octopus in the center.

Add the remaining marinade to the ridged grill pan and heat gently for 2 minutes. Toss the cucumber through the marinade to warm, then spoon over the salad.

Serves 4

Miso yakitori chicken

3 tablespoons yellow or red miso
  paste
2 tablespoons sugar
¼ cup sake
2 tablespoons mirin
2 lbs. boneless chicken thighs,
  skin left on
1 cucumber
2 scallions, cut into ¾-in. pieces

Soak twelve long, wooden bamboo skewers in cold water for at least 10 minutes. Place the miso, sugar, sake, and mirin in a small saucepan over medium heat and cook, stirring well, for 2 minutes or until the sauce is smooth and the sugar has dissolved completely.

Cut the chicken into 1-in. cubes. Seed the cucumber and cut into 1-in. batons. Thread the chicken, cucumber, and scallion pieces alternately onto the skewers—you should have three pieces of chicken, three pieces of cucumber, and three pieces of scallion per skewer.

Cook on a ridged grill pan over high heat, turning occasionally, for 10 minutes or until the chicken is almost cooked. Brush with the miso sauce and continue cooking, then turn and brush the other side. Repeat this process once or twice until the chicken and vegetables are cooked. Serve immediately with rice and salad.

Serves 4

Calamari and scallops with herb dressing

2 oranges
8 small calamari
6 oz. scallops, without roe
2 tablespoons vegetable oil
4 cups arugula
3 ripe Roma (plum) tomatoes,
  chopped

Herb dressing
1 cup finely chopped cilantro
1 cup finely chopped Italian parsley
2 teaspoons ground cumin
1 teaspoon paprika
1/4 cup lime juice
1/4 cup olive oil

Remove the skin and white pith from the oranges. Use a sharp knife to cut between the membranes and divide into segments. Remove the seeds.

To clean the squid, gently pull the tentacles away from the tubes. Remove the intestines from the tentacles by cutting under the eyes, then push out the beaks. Pull the quill from the tubes. Peel off the skin under cold running water. Wash the tubes and tentacles and place in a bowl of water with 1/4 teaspoon salt and mix. Cover and chill for about 30 minutes. Drain and cut the tubes into long strips and the tentacles into pieces.

Pull any membrane, vein, or hard white muscle from the scallops. Rinse and pat dry.

Heat the oil in a large, deep frying pan over high heat and cook the squid in batches for 1–2 minutes or until it turns white. Do not overcook or it will be tough. Drain on paper towels. Add the scallops to the pan and cook for 1–2 minutes each side or until tender.

Arrange the arugula on a large platter and top with seafood, tomatoes, and orange segments. Whisk the dressing ingredients together and pour over the seafood.

Serves 4

Lamb pitas with fresh mint salad

2 lbs. lean ground lamb
1 cup finely chopped parsley
1/2 cup finely chopped mint
1 onion, finely chopped
1 garlic clove, crushed
1 egg
1 teaspoon chili sauce
4 small whole-wheat pita pockets

Mint salad
3 small vine-ripened tomatoes
1 small red onion, finely sliced
1 cup mint
1 tablespoon olive oil
2 tablespoons lemon juice

plain yogurt (optional)

Place the lamb, parsley, mint, onion, garlic, egg, and chili sauce in a bowl and mix together. Shape into eight small patties. Chill for 30 minutes. Preheat the oven to 315°F.

To make the mint salad, slice the tomatoes into thin rings and place in a bowl with the onion, mint, olive oil, and lemon juice. Season well with salt and pepper. Gently toss to coat.

Wrap the pita pockets in aluminum foil and warm in the oven for 5 minutes.

Heat a ridged, cast-iron grill pan and brush with a little oil. When very hot, cook the patties for 3 minutes on each side. Do not turn until a nice crust has formed on the bottom or they will fall apart.

Remove the pitas from the oven. Cut the pockets in half, fill each half with some mint salad and a lamb patty. Serve with some plain yogurt if desired.

Serves 4

Blackened chicken with crispy tortillas

4 vine-ripened tomatoes, cut into
 $1/2$-in. slices
1 teaspoon sugar
1 red onion, sliced
$1/2$ cup plus 1 tablespoon olive oil
1 ripe avocado
$1/4$ cup sour cream
$1/3$ cup milk
2 tablespoons lime juice
2 corn tortillas (6-in. diameter)
1 teaspoon dried oregano
$2 1/2$ teaspoons ground cumin
$1 1/4$ teaspoons garlic salt
$1/2$ teaspoon cayenne pepper
4 small skinless, boneless chicken
 breasts (about $1 1/4$ lbs.)
$1/2$ cup cilantro

Place the tomato slices in a wide dish, sprinkle with sugar, and season well. Layer the onion over the top and drizzle with $1/4$ cup of oil. Chill for 20 minutes.

Blend the avocado, sour cream, milk, lime juice, and $1/3$ cup water in a food processor for 1 minute or until smooth. Season.

Cut each of the corn tortillas into eight $3/4$-in. strips. Combine the oregano, cumin, garlic salt, and cayenne pepper and coat the chicken breasts in the spice mixture, pressing down firmly with your fingers. Heat $1 1/2$ tablespoons of oil over medium-high heat in a large, nonstick frying pan until hot. Cook the chicken breasts for 4–5 minutes on each side or until cooked through. Cool, then refrigerate. In the same pan add $1/4$ cup of oil. Fry the tortilla strips until golden, turning once during cooking.

On each plate, arrange the tomato and onion slices in a small circle. Slice each chicken breast diagonally into $3/4$-in. pieces and arrange over the tomato. Spoon the dressing over the chicken and arrange four tortilla strips over the top. Sprinkle with cilantro and serve immediately.

Serves 4

Salmon fillets with lemon hollandaise sauce

Lemon hollandaise sauce
¾ cup butter
4 egg yolks
2 tablespoons lemon juice

2 tablespoons olive oil
4 salmon fillets, skin left on

Melt the butter in a small saucepan over low heat. Skim any froth from the surface and discard. Allow to cool. Whisk the yolks and 2 tablespoons water in a separate small saucepan for 30 seconds or until pale and foamy. Place the saucepan over very low heat and whisk the egg mixture for 2–3 minutes or until it is frothy and the whisk leaves a trail behind it as you whisk. Don't let the saucepan get too hot or you will scramble the eggs. Remove from the heat.

Add the cooled butter to the eggs, a little at a time, whisking well after each addition. Avoid using the milky whey from the bottom of the saucepan. Stir in the lemon juice and season with salt and cracked pepper.

Heat the oil in a large, nonstick frying pan over high heat and cook the salmon fillets, skin-side down, for 2 minutes. Turn over and cook for 2 minutes or until cooked to your liking. Serve with the sauce and vegetables of your choice.

Serves 4

Spaghetti Niçoise

12 oz. spaghetti
8 quail eggs (or 4 hen eggs)
1 lemon
3 (6-oz.) cans good-quality tuna in oil
1/3 cup pitted and halved Kalamata olives
2/3 cup sun-dried tomatoes, halved lengthwise
4 anchovy fillets, chopped into small pieces
3 tablespoons baby capers, drained
3 tablespoons chopped Italian parsley

Cook the pasta in a large saucepan of boiling water until al dente. Meanwhile, place the eggs in a saucepan of cold water, bring to a boil, and cook for 4 minutes (10 minutes for hen eggs). Drain, cool under cold water, then peel. Cut the quail eggs into halves or the hen eggs into quarters. Finely grate the zest of the lemon to give 1 teaspoon of grated zest. Then squeeze the lemon to give 2 tablespoons juice.

Empty the tuna and its oil into a large bowl. Add the olives, tomato halves, anchovies, lemon zest and juice, capers, and 2 tablespoons of the parsley. Drain the pasta and rinse in a little cold water, then toss gently through the tuna mixture. Divide among the serving bowls, garnish with egg halves or quarters and the remaining parsley, and serve.

Serves 4–6

Smoked chicken and pasta salad with mustard dressing

1 tablespoon balsamic vinegar
½ cup plus 1 tablespoon olive oil
1 tablespoon lemon juice
3 tablespoons whole-grain mustard
6 oz. bucatini pasta
1 lb. good-quality smoked chicken breast
8 small radishes
2 small Fuji apples
4 scallions, finely sliced
1 cup arugula

Combine the vinegar, olive oil, lemon juice, and mustard in a screw-top jar and shake well to combine. Season to taste with salt and pepper. Bring a large saucepan of salted water to a boil and cook the bucatini according to the package instructions until al dente. Drain, rinse under cold water, and drain again. Toss one third of the dressing through the bucatini and set aside for 30 minutes.

Cut the chicken breast diagonally and place in a large bowl. Thinly slice the radishes and add to the chicken. Quarter, core, and cube the apples without peeling them and add to the chicken with the sliced scallions and arugula. Pour in the remaining dressing and toss lightly.

Gently mix the pasta with the smoked chicken until well combined. Divide the salad among four serving dishes and serve with fresh, crusty bread. May be served cold as a light meal or appetizer.

Serves 4

Notes: Bucatini is a thick, spaghetti-like pasta with a hollow center. It has a chewy texture.
Smoked chicken often has a dark skin. You may wish to remove this to improve the appearance of the salad.

Prosciutto and vegetable pasta bake

3 tablespoons olive oil
⅓ cup dried breadcrumbs
8 oz. pasta shapes
6 thin slices prosciutto, chopped
1 red onion, chopped
1 red pepper, chopped
½ cup sun-dried tomatoes, roughly chopped
3 tablespoons shredded basil
1 cup grated fresh Parmesan cheese
4 eggs, lightly beaten
1 cup milk

Preheat the oven to 350°F. Grease a 10-in. round ovenproof dish with a little of the olive oil and sprinkle the dish with 2 tablespoons of the breadcrumbs to coat the bottom and side. Cook the pasta in a large saucepan of boiling water until al dente. Drain and transfer to a large bowl.

Heat 1 tablespoon of the remaining oil in a large frying pan. Add the prosciutto and onion and cook over medium heat for 4–5 minutes or until softened and golden in color. Add the pepper and sun-dried tomatoes and cook for another 1–2 minutes. Add to the pasta with the basil and Parmesan and toss together. Spoon the mixture into the prepared dish.

Place the eggs and milk in a bowl, whisk together, then season with salt and pepper. Pour the egg mixture over the pasta. Season the remaining breadcrumbs, add the remaining oil, and toss together. Sprinkle the seasoned breadcrumb mixture over the pasta. Bake for 40 minutes or until set. Allow to rest for 5 minutes, then cut into wedges and serve with a green salad if desired.

Serves 6–8

Tuna and white bean salad

12-oz. tuna steak
1 small red onion, thinly sliced
1 tomato, seeded and chopped
1 small red pepper, thinly sliced
2 (13-oz.) cans cannellini beans
2 garlic cloves, crushed
1 teaspoon chopped thyme
4 tablespoons finely chopped
  Italian parsley
1 1/2 tablespoons lemon juice
1/3 cup extra-virgin olive oil
1 teaspoon honey
olive oil, for brushing
3 cups arugula
1 teaspoon lemon zest

Place the tuna steak on a plate, sprinkle with cracked black pepper on both sides, cover with plastic, and refrigerate until needed.

Combine the onion, tomato, and pepper in a large bowl. Rinse the cannellini beans under cold running water for 30 seconds, drain, and add to the bowl with the garlic, thyme, and 3 tablespoons of the parsley.

Place the lemon juice, oil, and honey in a small saucepan, bring to a boil, then simmer, stirring, for 1 minute or until the honey dissolves. Remove from the heat.

Brush a barbecue or ridged cast-iron grill pan with olive oil and heat until very hot. Cook the tuna for 1 minute on each side. The meat should still be pink in the middle. Slice into 1 1/4-in. cubes and add to the salad. Pour on the warm dressing and toss well.

Place the arugula on a platter. Top with the salad, season, and garnish with the zest and remaining parsley.

Serves 4–6

Thai noodle salad

Dressing
2 tablespoons grated fresh ginger
2 tablespoons soy sauce
2 tablespoons sesame oil
1/3 cup red wine vinegar
1 tablespoon sweet chili sauce
2 garlic cloves, crushed
1/3 cup kecap manis

1 lb. cooked jumbo shrimp
8 oz. dried instant egg noodles
5 scallions, sliced diagonally
2 tablespoons chopped cilantro
1 red pepper, diced
1/4 lb. snow peas, sliced

For the dressing, whisk together the fresh ginger, soy sauce, sesame oil, red wine vinegar, chili sauce, garlic, and kecap manis in a large bowl.

Peel the shrimp and gently pull out the dark vein from each shrimp back, starting at the head. Cut each shrimp in half lengthwise.

Cook the egg noodles in a saucepan of boiling water for 2 minutes or until tender, then drain thoroughly. Cool in a large bowl.

Add the dressing, shrimp, and remaining ingredients to the noodles and toss gently. Can be served with lime wedges.

Serves 4

Shrimp and fennel salad

2 lbs. raw jumbo shrimp, peeled and deveined
1 large ($\frac{3}{4}$-lb.) fennel bulb, thinly sliced
10 cups watercress
2 tablespoons finely chopped chives
$\frac{1}{2}$ cup extra-virgin olive oil
$\frac{1}{4}$ cup lemon juice
1 tablespoon Dijon mustard
1 large garlic clove, finely chopped

Bring a saucepan of water to a boil, then add the shrimp, return to a boil, and simmer for 2 minutes or until the shrimp turn pink and are cooked through. Drain and allow to cool. Pat the shrimp dry with paper towels and slice in half lengthwise. Place in a large serving bowl.

Add the fennel, watercress, and chives to the bowl and mix well.

To make the dressing, whisk the oil, lemon juice, mustard, and garlic together until combined. Pour the dressing over the salad, season with salt and cracked black pepper, and toss gently. Arrange the salad on serving plates and serve immediately.

Serves 4

Somen noodle salad with sesame dressing

Sesame dressing
1/3 cup sesame seeds, toasted
2 1/2 tablespoons shoyu or light
  soy sauce
2 tablespoons rice vinegar
2 teaspoons sugar
1/2 teaspoon grated fresh ginger
1/2 teaspoon dashi granules

4 oz. dried somen noodles
1/4 lb. snow peas, finely sliced
  diagonally
1/4 lb. daikon radish, julienned
1 small carrot, julienned
1 scallion, sliced diagonally
1 cup spinach leaves, trimmed
2 teaspoons toasted sesame seeds

To make the dressing, place the sesame seeds in a mortar and pestle and grind until fine and moist. Combine the soy sauce, rice vinegar, sugar, ginger, dashi granules, and 1/2 cup water in a small saucepan and bring to a boil over high heat. Reduce the heat to medium and simmer, stirring, for 2 minutes or until the dashi granules have dissolved. Remove from the heat. Allow to cool. Gradually combine with the ground sesame seeds, stirring to form a thick dressing.

Cook the noodles in a large saucepan of boiling water for 2 minutes or until tender. Drain, rinse under cold water, and cool completely. Cut into 4-in. pieces using scissors.

Place the snow peas in a large, shallow bowl with the daikon, carrot, scallion, spinach leaves, and noodles. Add the dressing and toss well to combine. Place in the refrigerator until ready to serve. Just before serving, sprinkle the toasted sesame seeds on top.

Serves 4

Barbecued tuna and Mediterranean vegetables

3/4 cup olive oil
3 garlic cloves, crushed
2 tablespoons sweet chili sauce
1 red pepper, cut into 1 1/4-in. pieces
1 yellow pepper, cut into 1 1/4-in. pieces
2 large zucchini, cut into 1/2-in. slices
2 long, thin eggplants, cut into 1/2-in. slices
olive oil, extra, for brushing
4 tuna steaks

Lemon and caper mayonnaise
1 egg yolk
1 teaspoon grated lemon zest
2 tablespoons lemon juice
1 small garlic clove, chopped
3/4 cup olive oil
1 tablespoon baby capers, rinsed and drained

Combine the olive oil, garlic, and sweet chili sauce. Add the pepper, zucchini, and eggplants, toss well, then marinate for 30 minutes.

For the mayonnaise, process the egg yolk, zest, lemon juice, and garlic in a food processor or blender until smooth. With the motor running, gradually add the oil in a thin, steady stream until the mixture thickens and is a creamy consistency. Stir in the capers and 1/2 teaspoon salt.

Heat the barbecue or a ridged cast-iron grill pan, brush with oil, and cook the drained vegetables for 5 minutes each side or until cooked through. Keep warm.

Brush the tuna steaks with extra oil and barbecue for 2–3 minutes each side or until just cooked (tuna should be rare in the center). Arrange the vegetables and tuna steaks on serving plates and serve with the lemon and caper mayonnaise.

Serves 4

Stracci with artichokes and broiled chicken

1 tablespoon olive oil
3 skinless, boneless chicken breasts
1 lb. stracci pasta
8 slices prosciutto
9-oz. jar artichokes in oil, drained and
    quartered, oil reserved
3/4 cup sun-dried tomatoes, thinly
    sliced
2 cups baby arugula
2–3 tablespoons balsamic vinegar

Lightly brush a ridged, cast-iron grill pan or frying pan with the oil and heat over high heat. Cook the chicken for 6–8 minutes each side or until cooked through. Cut diagonally into thin slices.

Cook the pasta in a large saucepan of boiling water until al dente.

Meanwhile, place the prosciutto on a lined broiler pan and cook under a hot broiler for 2 minutes each side or until crisp. Cool slightly and break into pieces. Drain the pasta, then combine with the chicken, prosciutto, artichokes, tomatoes, and arugula in a bowl and toss. Whisk together 1/4 cup of the reserved artichoke oil and the balsamic vinegar and toss through the pasta mixture. Season to taste with salt and cracked pepper, then serve.

Serves 6

Goat cheese tart

Pastry
1 cup all-purpose flour
¼ cup olive oil

Filling
1 tablespoon olive oil
2 onions, thinly sliced
1 teaspoon thyme leaves
½ cup ricotta cheese
3½ oz. goat cheese
2 tablespoons pitted Niçoise olives
1 egg, lightly beaten
¼ cup whipping cream

For the pastry, sift the flour and a pinch of salt into a large bowl and make a well. Add the olive oil and mix with a flat-bladed knife until crumbly. Gradually add 3–4 tablespoons cold water until the mixture comes together. Remove and pat together to form a disk. Chill for 30 minutes.

For the filling, heat the olive oil in a frying pan. Add the onions, cover, and cook over low heat for 30 minutes. Season and stir in half the thyme. Cool slightly.

Preheat the oven to 350°F. Lightly flour the work surface and roll out the pastry to a 12-in. circle. Evenly spread the onion over the pastry, leaving a ¾-in. border. Sprinkle the ricotta and the goat cheese evenly over the onions. Place the olives over the cheeses, then sprinkle with the remaining thyme. Fold the pastry border in to the edge of the filling, gently pinching as you go.

Combine the egg and cream, then carefully pour over the filling. Bake on a heated cookie sheet on the lower half of the oven for 45 minutes or until the pastry is golden. Serve warm or at room temperature.

Serves 6

Chermoula shrimp

Chermoula

⅓ cup virgin olive oil
3 tablespoons chopped cilantro
2 tablespoons chopped Italian parsley
2 tablespoons chopped preserved
  lemon rind
2 tablespoons lemon juice
2 garlic cloves, chopped
1 small red chili, seeded and finely
  chopped
1 teaspoon ground cumin
½ teaspoon paprika

20 medium shrimp
2 cups instant couscous
1½ cups boiling chicken stock
1 tablespoon olive oil
2 tablespoons shredded mint leaves

Process the chermoula ingredients to a coarse puree, then season with salt.

Peel and devein the shrimp, keeping the tails intact. Thread a skewer or toothpick through the body of each shrimp to keep them straight, then place them in a dish and spoon the chermoula over them, turning to coat. Chill the shrimp, covered, for 30 minutes, turning occasionally.

Place the couscous in a heatproof bowl, pour on the boiling stock and oil, cover, and leave for 3–4 minutes. Fluff the couscous with a fork and stir in the mint.

Arrange the shrimp on a foil-lined grill pan and cook under a hot broiler for 2–3 minutes each side or until pink and cooked. Divide the couscous and shrimp among four serving plates.

Serves 4

Pan bagnat

4 crusty bread rolls, or 1 baguette
   sliced into four chunks
1 garlic clove
1/4 cup olive oil
1 tablespoon red wine vinegar
3 tablespoons basil leaves, torn
2 tomatoes, sliced
2 hard-boiled eggs, sliced
3-oz. can tuna
8 anchovy fillets
1 small cucumber, sliced
1/2 green pepper, thinly sliced
1 shallot, thinly sliced

Slice the bread rolls in half and remove some of the soft center from the tops. Cut the garlic clove in half and rub the insides of the rolls with the cut sides. Sprinkle both sides of the bread with olive oil, vinegar, salt, and pepper.

Place all the salad ingredients on the bottom of the rolls, cover with the other half, and wrap each sandwich in aluminum foil. Press firmly with a light weight, such as a can of soup, and leave in a cool place for 1 hour before serving.

Serves 4

Salmon with miso and soy noodles

10 oz. soba noodles
1 tablespoon soybean oil
1 tablespoon white miso paste
½ cup honey
1½ tablespoons sesame oil
6 salmon fillets, bones and skin
  removed
1 teaspoon chopped garlic
1 tablespoon grated fresh ginger
1 carrot, julienned
6 small scallions, thinly sliced
1 cup soybean sprouts
⅓ cup rice vinegar
3 tablespoons light soy sauce
1 teaspoon sesame oil, extra
1 tablespoon toasted sesame seeds

mustard cress

Preheat the oven to 350°F. Fill a large saucepan three-quarters full with water and bring to a boil. Add the soba noodles and return to a boil. Cook for 1 minute, then add 1 cup cold water. Boil for 1–2 minutes, then add another 1 cup water. Boil for 2 minutes or until tender, then drain and toss with ½ teaspoon of the soybean oil.

Combine the miso, honey, sesame oil, and 1 tablespoon water to form a paste. Brush over the salmon, then sear on a hot, ridged, cast-iron grill pan for 30 seconds on each side. Brush the salmon with the remaining paste and place on a baking sheet. Bake for 6 minutes, then cover and rest in a warm place.

Heat the remaining soy oil in a wok. Add the garlic, ginger, carrot, scallion, and sprouts and stir-fry for 1 minute— the vegetables should not brown, but remain crisp and bright. Add the noodles, rice vinegar, soy sauce, and extra sesame oil and stir-fry quickly to heat through.

Divide the noodles among six serving plates and top with a portion of salmon and sprinkle with the sesame seeds. Garnish with the mustard cress and serve.

Serves 6

Sides

Greek salad

4 tomatoes, cut into wedges
1 cucumber, peeled, halved, seeded,
   and cut into small cubes
2 green peppers, seeded, halved
   lengthwise, and cut into strips
1 red onion, finely sliced
16 Kalamata olives
1³/₄ cups firm feta cheese, cut into
   cubes
3 tablespoons Italian parsley
12 whole mint leaves
½ cup olive oil
2 tablespoons lemon juice
1 garlic clove, crushed

Place the tomato wedges, cucumber, pepper strips, onion, Kalamata olives, feta, and half of the parsley and mint leaves in a large serving bowl and toss together gently.

Place the oil, lemon juice, and garlic in a screw-top jar, season, and shake until well combined. Pour the dressing over the salad and toss. Garnish with the remaining parsley and mint.

Serves 4

Tuscan bread salad

6 oz. ciabatta bread
8 vine-ripened tomatoes
1/3 cup olive oil
1 tablespoon lemon juice
1 1/2 tablespoons red wine vinegar
6 anchovy fillets, finely chopped
1 tablespoon baby capers, rinsed,
   drained, and finely chopped
1 garlic clove, crushed
1 cup basil leaves

Preheat the oven to 425°F. Tear the bread into 3/4-in. pieces, arrange on a baking sheet, and bake for 5 minutes or until golden on the outside. Transfer the bread to a wire rack to cool.

Score a cross in the bottom of each tomato. Place in a heatproof bowl and cover with boiling water. Leave for 30 seconds, then transfer to cold water and peel the skin away from the cross. Cut four of the tomatoes in half and squeeze the juice and seeds into a bowl, reserving and chopping the flesh. Add the oil, juice, vinegar, anchovies, capers, and garlic to the tomato juice and season to taste.

Seed and slice the remaining tomatoes and place in a large bowl with the reserved tomatoes and most of the basil. Add the dressing and toasted bread and toss. Garnish with the remaining basil, season, and leave for at least 15 minutes. Serve at room temperature.

Serves 6

Grilled vegetable salad with balsamic dressing

4 baby eggplants
5 Roma (plum) tomatoes
2 red peppers
1 green pepper
2 zucchini
1/2 cup olive oil
12 baby bocconcini or small, fresh
  mozzarella
1/2 cup Ligurian olives
1 garlic clove, finely chopped
3 teaspoons baby capers, rinsed
  and drained
1/2 teaspoon sugar
2 tablespoons balsamic vinegar

Cut the eggplants and tomatoes in half lengthwise. Cut the red and green peppers in half lengthwise, remove the seeds and membrane, then cut each half into three pieces. Thinly slice the zucchini diagonally.

Preheat a ridged, cast-iron grill pan until hot. Add 1 tablespoon of oil and cook a quarter of the vegetables (cook the tomatoes cut-side down first) for 2–3 minutes or until seared and golden. Place in a large bowl.

Cook the remaining vegetables in batches until tender, adding more oil as needed. Transfer to the bowl and add the baby bocconcini. Mix the olives, garlic, capers, sugar, vinegar, and remaining oil (about 2 tablespoons). Pour over the salad and toss. Season with pepper.

Serves 4–6

Green salad with lemon vinaigrette

small head romaine lettuce
small head Bibb lettuce
1 1/2 cups watercress
3 cups arugula
1 tablespoon finely chopped shallots
2 teaspoons Dijon mustard
1/2 teaspoon sugar
1 tablespoon finely chopped basil
1 teaspoon grated lemon zest
3 teaspoons lemon juice
1 tablespoon white wine vinegar
1 1/2 tablespoons lemon oil
1/3 cup virgin olive oil

Remove the outer leaves from the lettuce heads and separate the core leaves. Wash in cold water, place in a colander to drain, then refrigerate. Pinch or trim the stems from the watercress and arugula, pat dry in a dishtowel, and chill with the lettuce.

To make the dressing, whisk together the shallots, mustard, sugar, basil, lemon zest, lemon juice, and vinegar in a bowl until well blended. Place the oils in a small bowl and slowly add to the bowl in a thin stream, whisking constantly to create a smooth, creamy dressing. Season to taste with salt and pepper.

Place the lettuce leaves in a large bowl. Drizzle the dressing over the salad and toss gently to coat.

Serves 6

Mushroom and goat cheese salad

Dressing
2 tablespoons lemon juice
3 tablespoons olive oil
1 teaspoon grated lemon zest

8 large cap mushrooms, stems
    removed
1 tablespoon chopped thyme
4 garlic cloves, finely chopped
2 tablespoons olive oil
2 cups baby arugula
3 oz. goat cheese
2 tablespoons chopped Italian parsley

Preheat the oven to 400°F. For the dressing, combine the juice, oil, and zest in a small bowl.

Place the mushrooms on a large baking sheet, sprinkle with thyme and garlic, then drizzle with olive oil. Cover with aluminum foil and roast for 20 minutes. Remove the mushrooms from the oven and toss to combine the flavors. Re-cover and roast for another 10 minutes or until cooked. Remove the mushrooms from the oven and cut in half.

Place the arugula on a serving platter, top with the mushrooms, and crumble the goat cheese over the top. Whisk the dressing to ensure it is well combined and drizzle over the salad. Serve sprinkled with parsley.

Serves 4–6

Roasted tomato and bocconcini salad

8 Roma (plum) tomatoes, halved
pinch of sugar
1/2 cup olive oil
1/4 cup torn basil
2 tablespoons balsamic vinegar
12 oz. cherry bocconcini or small, fresh mozzarella
5 handfuls mizuna lettuce

sea salt

Preheat the oven to 300°F. Place the tomatoes, cut-side up, on a rack over a baking tray lined with baking parchment. Sprinkle with salt, cracked black pepper, and a pinch of sugar. Roast for 2 hours, then remove from the oven and allow to cool.

Combine the oil and basil in a saucepan and stir gently over medium heat for 3–5 minutes or until it is very hot, but not smoking. Remove from the heat and discard the basil. Mix 2 tablespoons of oil with the vinegar.

Toss together the tomatoes, bocconcini, and lettuce. Arrange the salad in a shallow serving bowl and drizzle with the dressing. Sprinkle with sea salt and cracked black pepper.

Serves 6

Notes: If cherry bocconcini are unavailable, use regular bocconcini cut into quarters.
Leftover basil oil can be stored in a clean jar in the refrigerator and is great in pasta sauces.

Caramelized onion and potato salad

vegetable oil, for cooking
6 red onions, thinly sliced
2 lbs. new potatoes, unpeeled
4 slices bacon
2/3 cup chives, snipped

Mayonnaise dressing
1 cup mayonnaise
1 tablespoon Dijon mustard
juice of 1 lemon
2 tablespoons sour cream

Heat 2 tablespoons of oil in a large, heavy-bottomed frying pan, add the onions, and cook over medium-low heat for 40 minutes or until soft and caramelized.

Cut the potatoes into large chunks (if they are small, leave them whole). Cook in boiling water for 10 minutes or until just tender, then drain and cool slightly. (Do not overcook the potatoes or they will fall apart.)

Broil the bacon until crisp, drain on paper towels, and cool slightly before coarsely chopping.

Put the potatoes, onions, and chives in a large bowl, reserving a few chives for a garnish, and mix well.

To make the mayonnaise dressing, put the mayonnaise, mustard, lemon juice, and sour cream in a bowl and whisk to combine. Pour over the salad and toss to coat. Sprinkle with the bacon and garnish with the reserved chives.

Serves 10

Spinach salad with bacon and quail eggs

12 quail eggs
2 teaspoons vegetable oil
4 slices bacon, cut into thin strips
7 cups spinach leaves
$1/2$ lb. cherry tomatoes, halved
$2/3$ cup pine nuts, toasted

Dressing
$1/4$ cup apple cider vinegar
3 garlic cloves, crushed
2 teaspoons Dijon mustard
2 teaspoons maple syrup
1 teaspoon Worcestershire sauce
$1/4$ cup olive oil

Bring a small saucepan of water to a boil, gently add the quail eggs, and simmer for $1 1/2$ minutes. Drain, then rinse under cold running water until cool and peel the eggs.

Heat the oil in a nonstick frying pan over medium heat, add the bacon, and cook for 5–6 minutes or until crisp. Drain on paper towels, retaining the drippings in the pan.

Wash the spinach in cold water and remove the stems. Wrap the leaves loosely in a clean dishtowel to remove any excess water. Place in a salad bowl, tearing the larger leaves if necessary, then add the tomatoes, bacon, and pine nuts. Halve the eggs and sprinkle over the salad.

Reheat the bacon fat over medium heat, then add the vinegar, garlic, mustard, maple syrup, and Worcestershire sauce. Shake the pan over the heat for 2 minutes or until bubbling, then add the oil and heat for another minute. Pour the warm dressing over the salad, season to taste, and serve.

Serves 4–6

Tabbouleh

1 cup bulgur
large bunch Italian parsley, or small
   bunch curly parsley and 3 cups
   arugula
1¾ cups mint leaves
6 scallions, finely sliced
2 tomatoes, finely chopped
2 large garlic cloves, finely chopped
⅓ cup lemon juice
½ cup extra-virgin olive oil

Place the bulgur in a large bowl and add enough hot water to cover. Allow to soak for 15–20 minutes or until tender. Drain well.

Finely chop the parsley and mint and combine in a large bowl with the drained bulgur, scallions, and chopped tomatoes.

Mix the garlic and lemon juice together in a small bowl. Whisk in the oil until it is well combined, then season to taste with salt and black pepper. Toss the dressing through the salad before serving.

Serves 6–8

Variation: Add ¼ cup toasted pine nuts with the bulgur.

Fresh beet and goat cheese salad

2 lbs. fresh beets with leaves
1/2 lb. green beans
1 tablespoon red wine vinegar
2 tablespoons extra-virgin olive oil
1 garlic clove, crushed
1 tablespoon capers in brine, rinsed, drained, and coarsely chopped
3 oz. goat cheese

Trim the leaves from the beets. Scrub the bulbs and wash the leaves well. Bring a large saucepan of water to a boil, add the beets, then reduce the heat and simmer, covered, for 30 minutes or until tender when pierced with the point of a knife. (The cooking time may vary depending on the size of the bulbs.) Drain and cool. Peel the skins off the beets and cut the bulbs into wedges.

Meanwhile, bring a saucepan of water to a boil, add the beans, and cook for 3 minutes or until just tender. Remove with tongs and plunge into a bowl of cold water. Drain well. Add the beet leaves to the boiling water and cook for 3–5 minutes or until the leaves and stems are tender. Drain, plunge into a bowl of cold water, then drain again.

To make the dressing, put the vinegar, oil, garlic, capers, 1/2 teaspoon salt, and 1/2 teaspoon cracked black pepper in a jar and shake well. Divide the beans and beet wedges and leaves among four plates. Crumble the goat cheese over the top and drizzle with the dressing.

Serves 4

Watercress, feta, and watermelon salad

2 tablespoons sunflower seeds
1 lb. watermelon, rind removed, cut
  into ½-in. cubes
1⅓ cups feta cheese, cut into
  ½-in. cubes
2½ cups watercress sprigs
2 tablespoons olive oil
1 tablespoon lemon juice
2 teaspoons chopped oregano

Heat a small frying pan over high heat. Add the sunflower seeds and, shaking the pan continuously, dry-fry for 2 minutes or until they are toasted and lightly golden.

Place the watermelon, feta, and watercress sprigs in a large serving dish and toss gently to combine. Combine the olive oil, lemon juice, and chopped oregano in a small bowl and season to taste with a little salt and freshly ground black pepper (don't add too much salt, as the feta is already quite salty). Pour the dressing over the salad and toss together well. Sprinkle with the toasted sunflower seeds and serve.

Serves 4

Pear and walnut salad with lime vinaigrette

1 small French baguette, cut into
  sixteen thin slices
vegetable oil, for brushing
1 garlic clove, cut in half
1 cup walnuts
3/4 cup ricotta cheese
12 handfuls mixed salad leaves
2 pears, cut into 3/4-in. cubes, mixed
  with 2 tablespoons lime juice

Lime vinaigrette
1/4 cup lime juice
3 tablespoons vegetable oil
2 tablespoons raspberry vinegar

Preheat the oven to 350°F. Brush the baguette slices with a little oil, rub with the cut side of the garlic, then place on a baking sheet. Bake for 10 minutes or until crisp and golden. Place the walnuts on a baking tray and roast for 5–8 minutes or until slightly browned—shake the tray to ensure even coloring. Allow to cool for 5 minutes.

To make the lime vinaigrette, whisk together the lime juice, oil, vinegar, 1 teaspoon salt, and 1/2 teaspoon freshly ground black pepper in a small bowl. Set aside until ready to use.

Spread some of the ricotta cheese on each crouton, then cook under a hot broiler for 2–3 minutes or until hot.

Place the mixed salad, pears, and walnuts in a bowl, add the vinaigrette, and toss through. Divide the salad among four serving bowls and serve with the ricotta cheese croutons.

Serves 4

Fava bean, mint, and bacon salad

1 1/4 lbs. frozen fava beans (see Notes)
5-oz. head Bibb or romaine lettuce,
  shredded
3/4 cup shredded mint
8 oz. Kasseler or pancetta
1 tablespoon olive oil
1 1/2 teaspoons Dijon mustard
1 teaspoon sugar
2 tablespoons white wine vinegar
1/4 cup extra-virgin olive oil
4 flatbreads to serve (e.g. pita breads)

Blanch the beans according to package instructions. Drain, rinse under cold water, and peel. Place in a large bowl with the lettuce and mint.

Slice the Kasseler into thick slices, then into 3/4-in. chunks. Heat the oil in a heavy-bottomed frying pan and cook the Kasseler for 3–4 minutes or until golden. Add to the bean mixture.

Combine the mustard, sugar, and vinegar in a bowl. Whisk in the extra-virgin olive oil until well combined and season with salt and freshly ground black pepper. Pile the salad onto fresh or lightly toasted flatbread to serve.

Serves 4

Notes: If they are in season, you may want to use fresh fava beans. You will need about 3 3/4 lbs. of beans in the pod to give 1 1/4 lbs. of beans. Boil the beans for 2 minutes and peel before using them.
Kasseler is a traditional German specialty. It is a cured and smoked loin of pork that comes in a single piece and should be available at good delicatessens.

Radicchio with figs and ginger vinaigrette

1 radicchio
1 small curly endive lettuce (see Note)
3 oranges
1/2 small red onion, thinly sliced into rings
8 small green figs, quartered
3 tablespoons extra-virgin olive oil
1 teaspoon red wine vinegar
1/8 teaspoon ground cinnamon
2 tablespoons orange juice
2 tablespoons very finely chopped glacé ginger with syrup
2 pomegranates, optional

Wash the radicchio and curly endive leaves in cold water and drain well. Tear any large leaves into pieces.

Peel and segment the oranges, discarding all of the pith. Place in a large bowl with the onion rings, salad leaves, and figs, reserving eight fig quarters.

Combine the olive oil, vinegar, cinnamon, orange juice, and ginger in a small bowl. Season to taste with salt and pepper. Pour over the salad and toss lightly.

Arrange the reserved figs in pairs over the salad. If you are using the pomegranates, slice them in half and scoop out the seeds with a spoon. Sprinkle these over the salad before serving.

Serves 4

Notes: Curly endive is also known as frisée lettuce.
For a delicious variation, replace the oranges and orange juice with mandarins and mandarin juice when in season.

Egg salad with creamy dressing

10 large eggs, at room temperature
1 egg yolk
3 teaspoons lemon juice
2 teaspoons Dijon mustard
¼ cup olive oil
¼ cup vegetable oil
2 tablespoons chopped dill
1½ tablespoons crème frâiche or sour cream
2 tablespoons baby capers, rinsed and drained
⅓ cup mustard cress

Place the eggs in a large saucepan of cold water. Bring to a boil and simmer gently for 10 minutes. Drain, then cool the eggs under cold running water. Remove the shells.

Place the egg yolk, lemon juice, and Dijon mustard in a food processor or blender and season with salt and freshly ground black pepper. With the motor running, slowly add the combined olive oil and safflower oil, drop by drop at first, then slowly increasing the amount to a thin, steady stream as the mixture thickens. When all of the oil has been added, place the mayonnaise in a large bowl and gently stir in the dill, crème frâiche, and capers.

Roughly chop the eggs and fold into the mayonnaise. Transfer the salad to a serving bowl and use scissors to cut the green tips from the mustard cress. Sprinkle them over the salad and serve.

Serves 4

Serving suggestion: Serve the salad on slices of toasted bruschetta, draped with smoked salmon and topped with the mustard cress and extra black pepper.

Moroccan eggplant with couscous

1 cup instant couscous
3/4 cup olive oil
1 onion, halved and sliced
1 eggplant
3 teaspoons ground cumin
1 1/2 teaspoons garlic salt
1/4 teaspoon ground cinnamon
1 teaspoon paprika
1/4 teaspoon ground cloves
1/4 cup butter
1/2 cup roughly chopped parsley

Place the couscous in a large bowl and add 1 1/2 cups boiling water. Leave for 10 minutes, then fluff up the grains with a fork.

Add 2 tablespoons of oil to a large frying pan and cook the onion for 8–10 minutes or until browned. Remove from the pan, retaining the remaining oil.

Cut the eggplant into 1/2-in. slices, then into quarters, and place in a large bowl. Combine the cumin, garlic salt, cinnamon, paprika, cloves, and 1/2 teaspoon salt and sprinkle over the eggplant, tossing until it is well coated. Add the remaining oil to the pan and reheat over medium heat. Cook the eggplant, turning once, for 20–25 minutes or until browned. Remove from the pan and cool.

Using the same pan, melt the butter, then add the couscous and cook for 2–3 minutes. Stir in the onion, eggplant, and parsley, allow to cool, then serve.

Serves 4

Lentil salad

$\frac{1}{2}$ brown onion
2 cloves
1$\frac{2}{3}$ cups puy lentils (see Note)
1 strip lemon zest
2 garlic cloves, peeled
1 fresh bay leaf
2 teaspoons ground cumin
2 tablespoons red wine vinegar
$\frac{1}{4}$ cup olive oil
1 tablespoon lemon juice
2 tablespoons mint leaves, finely
  chopped
3 scallions, finely chopped

Stud the onion with the cloves and place in a saucepan with the lentils, zest, garlic, bay leaf, 1 teaspoon cumin, and 3$\frac{1}{2}$ cups water. Bring to a boil and cook over medium heat for 25–30 minutes or until the water has been absorbed. Discard the onion, zest, and bay leaf. Reserve the garlic and chop finely.

Whisk together the vinegar, oil, juice, garlic, and remaining cumin. Stir through the lentils with the mint and scallions. Season well. Leave for 30 minutes to let the flavors absorb. Serve at room temperature.

Serves 4–6

Note: Puy lentils are small, green lentils from France. They are available dried from gourmet food stores.

Coleslaw

½ green cabbage
¼ red cabbage
3 carrots, coarsely grated
6 radishes, coarsely grated
1 red pepper, chopped
4 scallions, sliced
¼ cup chopped parsley
1 cup mayonnaise

Remove the hard core from the cabbages and shred the leaves with a sharp knife. Place in a large bowl and add the grated carrot, grated radish, red pepper, scallions, and parsley to the bowl.

Add the mayonnaise, season to taste with salt and freshly ground black pepper, and toss until well combined.

Serves 8–10

Note: Cover and refrigerate the chopped vegetables for up to 3 hours before serving. Add the mayonnaise just before serving.

Soba noodle salad with tahini dressing

1 1/2 cups green beans
8 oz. dry soba noodles
1 tablespoon tahini
1 small garlic clove, crushed
1 1/2 tablespoons rice vinegar
1 1/2 tablespoons olive oil
1/2 teaspoon sesame oil
1 teaspoon soy sauce
2 teaspoons sugar
2 scallions, finely sliced
3 teaspoons black sesame seeds

Trim the beans and cut diagonally into long strips. Place in a saucepan of boiling water and return to a boil for 2 minutes or until tender. Drain and rinse under cold running water. Drain again.

Cook the noodles in boiling water for 3–4 minutes or until they are tender. Drain and rinse under cold water, then drain again.

Combine the tahini, crushed garlic, rice vinegar, olive oil, sesame oil, soy sauce, sugar, and 2 teaspoons warm water in a screw-top jar. Shake well and season to taste.

Combine the beans, noodles, scallions, and sesame seeds in a serving bowl, add the dressing, and toss lightly to combine. Serve immediately.

Serves 4–6

Note: Add the dressing as close to serving as possible, as it will be absorbed by the noodles.

Insalata Caprese

3 large vine-ripened tomatoes
9 oz. bocconcini (see Note)
12 basil leaves
¼ cup extra-virgin olive oil
4 basil leaves, roughly torn, extra
  (optional)

Slice the tomatoes into ½-in. slices to make twelve slices altogether. Slice the bocconcini into twenty-four ½-in. slices.

Arrange the tomato slices on a serving plate, alternating them with two slices of bocconcini. Place the basil leaves between the slices of bocconcini.

Drizzle with the oil, sprinkle with the basil (if desired), and season well with salt and ground black pepper.

Serves 4

Note: This popular salad is most successful with very fresh buffalo mozzarella, if you can find it. We've used bocconcini in this recipe. These are small balls of fresh cow's-milk mozzarella.

Moroccan spiced carrot salad

4 large carrots
2 cardamom pods
1 teaspoon black mustard seeds
1/2 teaspoon ground cumin
1/2 teaspoon ground ginger
1 teaspoon paprika
1/2 teaspoon ground coriander
1/3 cup olive oil
1 tablespoon lemon juice
2 tablespoons orange juice
1/4 cup raisins
1/2 cup finely chopped cilantro
2 tablespoons finely chopped
   pistachio nuts
1 teaspoon orange flower water
1 cup plain yogurt

Peel and coarsely grate the carrots and place in a large bowl.

Crush the cardamom pods to extract the seeds. Discard the pods. Heat a frying pan over low heat and cook the mustard seeds for a few seconds or until they start to pop. Add the cumin, ginger, paprika, cardamom, and ground coriander and heat for 5 seconds or until fragrant. Remove from the heat and stir in the oil, juices, and raisins until combined.

Pour the dressing over the carrots and leave for 30 minutes. Add the cilantro and toss to combine. Pile the salad onto a serving dish and garnish with the chopped pistachios. Mix the orange flower water and yogurt and serve separately.

Serves 4–6

Mixed salad with warm Brie dressing

1/2 sourdough baguette
3/4 cup extra-virgin olive oil
6 slices bacon
2 garlic cloves, peeled
2 heads romaine lettuce
2 cups spinach leaves
1/2 cup pine nuts, toasted
2 French shallots, finely chopped
1 tablespoon Dijon mustard
1/3 cup sherry vinegar
10 oz. ripe Brie cheese, rind removed

Preheat the oven to 350°F. Thinly slice the baguette diagonally. Use 2 tablespoons of oil to brush both sides of each slice, place on a cookie sheet, and bake for 20 minutes or until golden.

Place the bacon on a separate sheet and bake for 3–5 minutes or until crisp. Remove the bread from the oven and use one clove of garlic to rub the bread slices. Break the bacon into pieces and leave to cool.

Remove the outer leaves of the lettuce. Rinse the inner leaves well, drain, dry, and place in a large bowl with the spinach. Add the bacon, croutons, and pine nuts.

Place the remaining olive oil in a frying pan and heat gently. Add the shallots and cook until they soften, then crush the remaining clove of garlic and add to the pan. Whisk in the mustard and vinegar, then gently whisk in the chopped Brie until it has melted. Remove the dressing from the heat and, while it is still warm, pour over the salad and toss gently.

Serves 4

Vegetable skewers with salsa verde

Salsa verde
1 garlic clove
1 tablespoon capers, rinsed
and drained
1 cup Italian parsley
1/2 cup basil leaves
1/2 cup mint leaves
1/3 cup olive oil
1 teaspoon Dijon mustard
1 tablespoon red wine vinegar

16 small yellow squash
16 baby carrots, peeled
16 French shallots, peeled
1 large red pepper, halved and cut
into 1-in.-thick slices
16 baby zucchini
2 garlic cloves, crushed
1 teaspoon chopped thyme
1 tablespoon olive oil
16 fresh bay or sage leaves

Soak sixteen wooden skewers in cold water for 30 minutes to keep them from burning during cooking.

To make the salsa verde, combine the garlic, capers, and herbs in a food processor until the herbs are roughly chopped. With the motor running, pour the olive oil in a slow stream until incorporated. Combine the mustard with the red wine vinegar and stir through the salsa verde. Season to taste. Cover with plastic wrap and refrigerate.

Blanch the vegetables separately in a large pot of boiling, salted water until just tender. Drain in a colander, then toss with the garlic, thyme, and oil. Season well.

Thread the vegetables onto the skewers starting with a squash, then a French shallot, a bay leaf, then the zucchini, carrot, and pepper. Repeat for all of the skewers.

Place the skewers on a hot grill and cook for 3 minutes on each side or until cooked and browned. Arrange on couscous or rice and serve with the salsa verde.

Serves 8

Roast tomato salad

6 Roma (plum) tomatoes
2 teaspoons capers, rinsed
  and drained
6 basil leaves, torn
1 tablespoon olive oil
1 tablespoon balsamic vinegar
2 garlic cloves, crushed
1/2 teaspoon honey

Cut the tomatoes lengthwise into quarters. Place on a grill tray, skin-side down, and broil for 4–5 minutes or until golden. Cool to room temperature and place in a bowl.

Combine the capers, basil leaves, olive oil, balsamic vinegar, garlic cloves, and honey in a bowl, season with salt and freshly ground black pepper, and pour over the tomatoes. Toss gently.

Serves 6

Bean salad

2 cups green beans, trimmed
2 cups yellow beans, trimmed
¼ cup olive oil
1 tablespoon lemon juice
1 garlic clove, crushed
shaved Parmesan cheese

Bring a saucepan of lightly salted water to a boil. Add the green and yellow beans and cook for 2 minutes or until just tender. Plunge into cold water and drain.

Place the olive oil, lemon juice, and garlic in a bowl, season with salt and freshly ground black pepper, and mix together well. Place the beans in a serving bowl, pour on the dressing, and toss to coat. Top with the Parmesan and serve.

Serves 6

Dill potato salad

1 1/3 lbs. red potatoes
2 eggs
2 tablespoons finely chopped dill
1 1/2 tablespoons finely chopped
  French shallots
1 egg yolk
2 teaspoons lemon juice
1 teaspoon Dijon mustard
1/2 cup light olive oil

Bring a large saucepan of water to a boil. Cook the potatoes for 20 minutes or until tender. Add the eggs for the last 10 minutes. Remove the potatoes and eggs and allow to cool. Peel the potatoes, then cut into 1-in. cubes. Peel and chop the eggs. Place in a large bowl with the dill, eggs, and shallots. Toss to combine, then season.

Place the egg yolk, lemon juice, mustard, and a pinch of salt in the bowl of a food processor. With the motor running, gradually add the olive oil a few drops at a time. When about half the oil has been added, pour in the remaining oil in a steady stream until it has all been incorporated. Use a large metal spoon to gently combine the potato and mayonnaise, then serve.

Serves 4

Beet and sweet potato salad with feta

12 oz. fresh beets, trimmed and
  washed
12 oz. orange sweet potatoes, peeled
  and cut into 1-in. chunks
¼ cup garlic oil (see Note)
1 garlic bulb
3 tablespoons olive oil
1½ tablespoons butter
1 red onion, cut into ½-in. wedges
1 tablespoon balsamic vinegar
1 teaspoon brown sugar
2 tablespoons lemon juice
1 tablespoon shredded basil
1 cup spinach leaves
2 sprigs rosemary, leaves removed
  and stems discarded
½ cup feta cheese

Preheat the oven to 350°F. Wrap each beet in foil and place on a cookie sheet. Brush the sweet potatoes with garlic oil and season. Place on another cookie sheet with the whole garlic bulb. Cook with the beet for 35–40 minutes or until tender. Test with a skewer and remove from the oven when tender. Allow to cool.

Heat 1 tablespoon of olive oil and the butter in a small saucepan over medium heat until the butter has melted. Add the onion and cook, stirring occasionally, for 15 minutes or until soft. Add the vinegar and sugar and cook for 3–5 minutes or until the onion is golden and starting to caramelize.

Peel the garlic cloves and combine them with the lemon juice, basil, and remaining oil. Season to taste.

Toss the spinach, beets, sweet potatoes, onion, and rosemary in a bowl. Crumble the feta over the top and drizzle with the dressing. Serve warm.

Serves 4

Note: If garlic oil is unavailable, you can make your own by steeping some crushed garlic in extra-virgin olive oil for 2 hours, then straining, or use plain olive oil.

Caponata

2 lbs. eggplant, cubed
3/4 cup olive oil
1 1/2 cups zucchini, cubed
1 red pepper, thinly sliced
2 onions, finely sliced
4 celery stalks, sliced
14-oz. can crushed tomatoes
3 tablespoons red wine vinegar
2 tablespoons sugar
2 tablespoons capers, rinsed
   and drained
24 green olives, pitted
2 tablespoons pine nuts, toasted

Put the eggplant in a colander, add 2 teaspoons of salt, and leave to drain.

Heat 3 tablespoons of the oil in a large frying pan and fry the zucchini and pepper for 5–6 minutes or until the zucchini is lightly browned. Transfer to a bowl. Add a little more oil to the pan and gently fry the onion and celery for 6–8 minutes or until softened but not brown. Transfer to the bowl with the zucchini.

Rinse the eggplant and pat dry. Add 1/4 cup of the oil to the pan, increase the heat, and brown the eggplant in batches. Keep adding more oil to each batch. Drain on paper towels and set aside.

Remove any excess oil from the pan and return the vegetables to the pan, except the eggplant.

Add 1/4 cup water and the tomatoes. Reduce the heat and simmer for 10 minutes. Add the remaining ingredients and eggplant and mix well. Remove from the heat and cool. Cover and leave for twenty-four hours in the refrigerator. Add some pepper, and more vinegar if needed.

Serves 8

Frisée and garlic crouton salad

Vinaigrette
1 French shallot, finely chopped
1 tablespoon Dijon mustard
¼ cup tarragon vinegar
⅔ cup extra-virgin olive oil

1 tablespoon olive oil
8 oz. bacon, cut into 1-in. pieces
½ baguette, sliced
4 garlic cloves
1 baby frisée (curly endive), washed and dried
½ cup walnuts, toasted

For the vinaigrette, whisk together in a bowl the shallot, mustard, and vinegar. Slowly add the oil, whisking constantly until thickened. Set aside.

Heat the oil in a large frying pan. Add the bacon, bread, and garlic cloves and cook over medium-high heat for 5–8 minutes or until the bread and bacon are both crisp. Remove the garlic from the pan.

Place the frisée, bread, bacon, walnuts, and vinaigrette in a large bowl. Toss together well and serve.

Serves 4–6

Sweets

Baked lemon cheesecake

½ cup crushed graham crackers
5 tablespoons butter, melted
1¼ cups low-fat ricotta cheese
¾ cup low-fat cream cheese
½ cup sugar
⅓ cup lemon juice
2 tablespoons grated lemon zest
1 egg
1 egg white

Preheat the oven to 315°F. Lightly grease an 8-in. springform pan and line the base with baking parchment. Combine the graham crackers and butter and press into the base of the pan. Refrigerate for 30 minutes.

Beat the ricotta, cream cheese, sugar, lemon juice, and 3 teaspoons of lemon zest with an electric beater until smooth. Beat in the egg and egg white.

Pour the mixture into the pan and sprinkle the surface with the remaining lemon zest. Bake for 45 minutes—the center will still be a little wobbly. Leave to cool, then chill for 5 hours before serving.

Serves 8

Orchard fruit compote

¼ cup honey
½ teaspoon ground ginger
1 cinnamon stick
3 whole cloves
pinch ground nutmeg
3 cups dessert wine, such as
  Sauternes
1 lemon
6 pitted prunes
3 dried peaches, halved
5 dates, seeded and halved
10 dried apricots
1 lapsang souchong tea bag
2 golden delicious apples
2 beurre bosc pears
1 cup plain yogurt

Place the honey, ginger, cinnamon stick, cloves, nutmeg, and wine in a saucepan. Peel a large piece of zest from the lemon and place in the pan. Squeeze the juice from the lemon to give ¼ cup and add to the pan. Bring to a boil, stirring, then simmer for 20 minutes.

Meanwhile, place the prunes, peaches, dates, and apricots in a large heatproof bowl. Cover with boiling water, add the tea bag, and leave to soak. Peel and core the apples and pears, then cut into pieces about the same size as the dried fruits. Add to the syrup and allow to simmer for 8–10 minutes or until tender. Drain the dried fruit and remove the tea bag, then add the fruit to the pan and cook for another 5 minutes.

Remove all the fruit from the pan with a slotted spoon and place in a serving dish. Return the pan to the heat, bring to a boil, then reduce the heat and simmer for 6 minutes or until the syrup has reduced by half. Pour over the fruit compote and chill for 30 minutes. Serve with the yogurt.

Serves 4

Berries in champagne jelly

4 cups champagne or sparkling
  white wine
1 1/2 tablespoons unflavored powdered
  gelatin
1 cup sugar
4 strips lemon zest
4 strips orange zest
1 2/3 cups small strawberries, hulled
  and halved
1 2/3 cups blueberries

Pour 2 cups champagne into a bowl and let the bubbles subside. Sprinkle the gelatin over the champagne in an even layer. Leave until the gelatin is spongy—do not stir. Place the remaining champagne in a large saucepan with the sugar, lemon and orange zest and heat gently, stirring constantly for 3–4 minutes or until all of the sugar has dissolved.

Remove the pan from the heat, add the gelatin mixture, and stir until thoroughly dissolved. Leave the jelly to cool completely, then remove the lemon and orange zest.

Divide the berries among eight 1/2-cup stemmed wine glasses and gently pour the jelly over the top. Refrigerate for 6 hours or overnight, until the jelly has fully set. Remove from the refrigerator 15 minutes before serving.

Serves 8

Macaroon berry trifle

1²/₃ cups skim milk
2 tablespoons sugar
1 teaspoon vanilla extract
2¹/₂ tablespoons custard powder
1 tablespoon Marsala
2 teaspoons instant coffee powder
16 amaretti cookies, roughly broken
2 tablespoons orange juice
1¹/₂ cups fresh raspberries
15-oz. can pears in natural juice,
   drained and roughly chopped

vanilla ice cream

Place the milk, sugar, and vanilla in a heavy-based saucepan and cook over low heat, stirring occasionally. Combine the custard powder with 2 tablespoons of water, mix to a smooth paste, and whisk into the milk mixture until the custard boils and thickens. Remove from the heat and cover with plastic wrap, placing it directly on the surface of the custard to keep any skin from forming, and allow to cool.

Place the Marsala and coffee powder in a small bowl and stir until the coffee has dissolved. Place the cookies and orange juice in a large bowl and stir to coat the cookies. Layer half of the cookies in the base of four serving glasses and drizzle with the Marsala mixture. Top with a third of the berries and half of the pears, then pour in half of the custard. Repeat the layering, finishing with the raspberries. Refrigerate the trifles for 10 minutes or serve immediately with a scoop of vanilla ice cream.

Serves 4

Chocolate and raspberry ice-cream sandwich

10-oz. frozen chocolate pound cake
2 tablespoons raspberry liqueur
(optional)
2 cups fresh or thawed raspberries
1 cup sugar
1 teaspoon lemon juice
1 quart vanilla ice cream, softened
confectioners' sugar, to dust

Using a sharp knife, cut the pound cake lengthwise into four thin slices. Using a 2½-in. cookie cutter, cut eight rounds from the slices of cake. You will need two rounds of cake per person. Brush each round with half of the raspberry liqueur (if using), then cover and set aside.

Line an 8-in.-square pan or dish with baking parchment, leaving a generous overhang of paper on two opposite sides. Place the raspberries, sugar, lemon juice, and remaining liqueur in a blender and blend to a smooth puree. Reserving ½ cup of the puree, fold the remainder through the ice cream and pour into the pan. Freeze for 2 hours or until firm.

Remove the ice cream from the freezer and use the overhanging paper to lift it from the pan. Using the 2½-in. cookie cutter, cut four rounds from the ice cream.

To assemble, place four slices of cake on a tray, and top each with a round of ice cream and then the remaining slices of cake. Smooth the sides of the ice cream to neaten, if necessary. Return the sandwiches to the freezer for 5 minutes to firm. Dust with confectioners' sugar and serve with the remaining raspberry sauce.

Serves 4

Mango sorbet

1½ cups sugar
½ cup lime juice
5 fresh mangoes (3 lbs.)

Place the sugar in a saucepan with 2½ cups water. Stir over low heat until the sugar dissolves, then bring to a boil. Reduce to a simmer for 15 minutes, then stir in the juice.

Peel the mangoes and remove the flesh from the pits. Chop and place in a heatproof bowl. Add the syrup and leave to cool.

Place the mango mixture in a blender, blend until smooth, then pour into a shallow metal dish and freeze for 1 hour or until it starts to freeze around the edges. Return to the blender and blend until smooth. Pour back into the tray and return to the freezer. Repeat three times. For the final freezing, place in an airtight container and cover the sorbet with a piece of waxed paper and lid. Allow the sorbet to soften slightly before serving with tropical fruit.

Serves 4

Note: You can use frozen mangoes if fresh mango is unavailable. Use 2 lbs. frozen mango (softened), ¾ cup sugar, and ¼ cup lime juice, and follow the method as above.

Lemongrass and ginger fruit salad

¼ cup sugar
1 x 1 in. piece fresh ginger, thinly
  sliced
1 stalk lemongrass, bruised and
  halved
1 large passion fruit
1 red papaya
½ honeydew melon
1 large mango
1 small fresh pineapple
12 fresh litchis
¼ cup mint leaves, shredded

Place the sugar, ginger, and lemongrass in a small saucepan, add ½ cup water, and stir over low heat to dissolve the sugar. Boil for 5 minutes or until reduced to ⅓ cup, then cool. Strain the syrup and add the passion fruit pulp.

Peel and seed the papaya and melon. Cut into 1½-in. cubes. Peel the mango and cut the flesh into cubes, discarding the pit. Peel, halve, and core the pineapple and cut into cubes. Peel the litchis, then make a slit in the flesh and remove the seeds.

Place all the fruit in a large serving bowl. Pour on the syrup, or serve separately if preferred. Garnish with the shredded mint.

Serves 4

Chocolate chip banana ice cream

2½ cups low-fat custard
2 ripe bananas, mashed
2 teaspoons lemon juice
1½ oz. dark chocolate

Combine the custard, mashed banana, and lemon juice in a large mixing bowl. Beat with an electric mixer until the banana and custard are well combined, with no lumps of banana remaining.

Pour into a metal cake pan, cover with plastic wrap, and freeze for 3–4 hours or until semifrozen. Transfer to a chilled bowl and beat for 2 minutes with an electric mixer until slushy, then return to the cake pan and place in the freezer for 2–3 hours or until almost firm. Repeat the freezing and beating twice more (for a total of three times).

Finely chop the chocolate and fold into the mixture after the last beating. Refreeze in an airtight plastic container. Remove from the freezer and allow the ice cream to soften slightly before serving.

Serves 6

Cassata

1 oz. crystallized ginger, finely
chopped
2 oz. red glacé cherries, roughly
chopped or sliced
1¼ cups low-fat vanilla ice cream,
softened
9 oz. frozen strawberry sorbet,
softened
1¼ cups low-fat chocolate ice cream,
softened

Line a 5-cup rectangular pan with
plastic wrap, leaving an overhang
on the sides.

Stir the ginger and glacé cherries
into the vanilla ice cream until well
combined. Spoon into the prepared
pan and smooth down. Freeze for
1 hour or until firm.

Spoon the strawberry sorbet over
the ice cream mixture, smooth the
surface, and return to the freezer for
another hour.

Spoon the chocolate ice cream
over the strawberry, smoothing the
surface. Cover with plastic wrap
and freeze for at least 3 hours or
overnight. To serve, plunge the
bottom of the pan into warm water
for 10 seconds to loosen, then lift
out using the plastic wrap. Cut into
slices and serve.

Serves 10–12

Summer dessert

1 cup black currants
1 cup red currants
1 cup raspberries
1 cup blackberries
1 1/2 cups strawberries, hulled and
   quartered or halved
1/2 cup sugar, or to taste
6–8 slices good-quality white bread,
   crusts removed

Put all the berries except the strawberries in a saucepan with 1/2 cup water and heat for 5 minutes or until the berries begin to soften. Add the strawberries and remove from the heat. Add sugar to taste (how much you need will depend on how ripe the fruit is). Allow to cool.

Line six 2/3-cup molds or a 4-cup baking dish with the bread. For the small molds, cut a circle to fit the bottom and strips to fit around the sides. For the dish, cut a large circle out of one slice for the bottom and cut the rest of the bread into strips to fit the side. Drain a little of the juice off the fruit. Dip one side of each piece of bread in the juice before fitting it, juice-side down, into the basin, leaving no gaps. Do not squeeze the bread or it will not absorb the juice.

Fill each mold with fruit and add some juice. Cover the top with the rest of the dipped bread, juice-side up. Cover with plastic wrap. For the small molds, put a small can on top of each. For the dish, set a small plate on the plastic wrap, then weigh it down with a large can. Place on a tray to catch any juice that may overflow, and chill overnight. Carefully turn out the dessert and serve with the leftover fruit and whipping cream if desired.

Serves 6

White chocolate mousse

3½ oz. white chocolate
½ cup skim milk
2 teaspoons unflavored powdered
  gelatin
2 cups low-fat French vanilla fromage
  frais or whipped cream
3 egg whites
3 tablespoons passion fruit pulp
confectioners' sugar, to dust

Place the chocolate and milk in a small saucepan and stir over low heat until the chocolate has melted. Allow to cool. Place ¼ cup boiling water in a heatproof bowl, sprinkle evenly with the gelatin, and stir until dissolved. Using a wooden spoon, stir the gelatin into the chocolate mixture.

Place the fromage frais in a large bowl and gradually stir in the chocolate mixture, a little at a time, stirring until smooth after each addition.

Beat the egg whites in a clean, dry bowl with electric beaters until soft peaks form. Gently fold the egg whites and the passion fruit pulp into the chocolate mixture. Divide the mixture equally among eight ½-cup serving dishes or a 4-cup glass bowl. Refrigerate for 3 hours or until set. Serve with a light dusting of confectioners' sugar.

Serves 8

Note: It is important to have the ingredients at room temperature to ensure that the texture is smooth.

Watermelon granita

1 cup sugar
3-lb. watermelon

Place the sugar in a saucepan with 1 cup water and stir over low heat without boiling until the sugar has completely dissolved. Increase the heat and bring to a boil, then reduce the heat and simmer, without stirring, for 5 minutes. Pour into a large bowl to cool.

Remove the rind from the watermelon and place chunks of flesh in a food processor. Process until pureed, then strain to remove the seeds and fiber. Mix the watermelon puree with the sugar syrup and pour into a shallow metal dish. Freeze for 1 hour or until just frozen around the edges. Scrape this back into the mixture with a fork.

Repeat scraping the frozen edges every hour, at least twice more or until the mixture has even-sized ice crystals. Serve immediately or beat well with a fork and refreeze just before serving. To serve, scrape the granita into serving dishes with a fork or serve in scoops in a tall glass.

Serves 4

Variation: For refreshing, extra flavor, add 2 tablespoons chopped mint when freezing the last time.

Almond semifreddo

1¼ cups cream
4 eggs, at room temperature,
  separated
²/₃ cup confectioners' sugar
¼ cup Amaretto liquer
½ cup blanched almonds, toasted
  and chopped
8 amaretti cookies, crushed

fresh fruit or extra Amaretto

Whip the cream until firm peaks form, then cover and chill. Line an 8 x 4 in. loaf pan with plastic wrap so that it overhangs the two long sides.

Place the confectioners' sugar and egg yolks in a large bowl and beat until pale and creamy. Whisk the egg whites in a separate bowl until firm peaks form. Stir the Amaretto, almonds, and amaretti cookies into the egg yolk mixture, then carefully fold in the chilled cream and the egg whites until well combined. Carefully pour or spoon into the lined loaf pan and cover with the overhanging plastic. Freeze for 4 hours or until frozen but not rock-hard. Serve in slices with fresh fruit or a sprinkling of Amaretto. The semifreddo can also be poured into individual molds or serving dishes before freezing.

Serves 8–10

Note: Semifreddo means "semifrozen," so if you want to leave it in the freezer overnight, remove it and place it in the refrigerator for 30 minutes to soften slightly before serving.

Petite custard tarts

3 ready-made piecrusts
1 cup skim milk
1 tablespoon custard powder
¼ cup sugar
1 teaspoon vanilla extract
⅓ cup passion fruit pulp
½ teaspoon unflavored powdered
  gelatin

Preheat the oven to 350°F. Cut twelve circles from the piecrusts using a 3-in. round cookie cutter. Gently press into twelve muffin cups (2½ in. diameter and 1 in. deep) and prick each round with a fork.

Cut out a 2-in. square of foil for each cup and press into the cup. Bake for 10 minutes, remove the foil, and bake for 5 minutes or until golden and cooked through. Cool on a rack.

Mix 1 tablespoon of the milk and the custard powder until smooth. Stir the sugar, vanilla, and remaining milk over medium heat for 1 minute or until the sugar dissolves. Stir in the custard mixture and cook, stirring, for 2–3 minutes or until thick. Cover the surface of the custard with plastic wrap. Cool to room temperature.

Place the passion fruit in a heatproof bowl and sprinkle with gelatin. Leave until the gelatin is spongy. Bring a saucepan of water to a boil, remove from the heat, and place the bowl in the pan. Stir until the gelatin dissolves, then leave to cool. Divide the custard among the muffin cups. Top each with 1 teaspoon of the passion fruit glaze and chill for at least 2 hours.

Makes 12

Individual zucotto

16-oz. Madeira cake
1/4 cup Cointreau
1/4 cup brandy
1 1/4 cups heavy cream
3 teaspoons confectioners' sugar,
  sifted
1/2 cup blanched almonds, roasted
  and roughly chopped
1/2 cup hazelnuts, roasted and roughly
  chopped
5 oz. good-quality dark chocolate,
  finely chopped

Cut the cake into 1/4-in. slices. Lightly grease six 1/2-cup ramekins and line with plastic wrap, leaving enough to hang over the sides. Press the pieces of the cake into the ramekins, overlapping to cover the base and sides. Combine the Cointreau and brandy in a bowl. Brush the cake with half the Cointreau mixture.

Place the cream and confectioners' sugar in a bowl, and, using electric beaters, beat until firm and stiff. Fold in the nuts, chocolate, and 1 1/2 teaspoons Cointreau mixture. The mixture will be quite stiff.

Spoon the mixture into each ramekin and smooth over the surface. Cover with the overhanging plastic wrap and refrigerate for 2 hours or overnight. To serve, use the plastic wrap to lift the zucotto out of the ramekins, turn upside down onto serving plates, and brush with the remaining Cointreau mixture.

Serves 6

Apple and pear sorbet

4 large green apples, peeled, cored, and chopped
4 pears, peeled, cored, and chopped
1 piece of lemon zest (2½ x ½ in.)
1 cinnamon stick
¼ cup lemon juice
4 tablespoons sugar
2 tablespoons Calvados or Poire William liqueur (optional)

Place the apple and pear in a large, deep saucepan with the lemon zest, cinnamon stick, and enough water to just cover the fruit. Cover and poach the fruit gently over medium-low heat for 6–8 minutes or until tender. Remove the lemon zest and cinnamon stick. Place the fruit in a food processor and blend with the lemon juice until smooth.

Place the sugar in a saucepan with ⅓ cup water, bring to a boil, and simmer for 1 minute. Add the fruit puree and the liqueur and combine.

Pour into a shallow metal tray and freeze for 2 hours or until the mixture is frozen around the edges. Transfer to a food processor or bowl and blend or beat until just smooth. Pour back into the tray and return to the freezer. Repeat this process three times. For the final freezing, place in an airtight container, cover the surface with a piece of waxed paper, and cover with a lid. Serve in small glasses or bowls.

Serves 4–6

Notes: Pour an extra nip of Calvados over the sorbet to serve, if desired.

Spiced poached pears

6 beurre bosc pears
1¼ cups rosé wine
¾ cup good-quality apple or
  pear juice
4 cloves
1 vanilla bean, halved
1 cinnamon stick
1 tablespoon maple syrup
1 cup low-fat vanilla yogurt

Peel, halve, and core the pears. Place in a deep frying pan with a lid and add the wine, fruit juice, and cloves. Scrape the seeds out of the vanilla bean and add both the seeds and pod to the pan. Stir in the cinnamon stick and maple syrup. Bring to a boil, then reduce the heat and simmer for 5–7 minutes or until the pears are tender. Remove from the heat and cover with a lid.

Leave the fruit for 30 minutes to allow the flavors to infuse, then remove the pears with a slotted spoon and place in a serving dish. Return the syrup to the heat and boil for 6–8 minutes or until reduced by half. Strain the syrup over the pears. Serve warm or chilled with the yogurt.

Serves 6

Ginger and litchi gelatin

20-oz. can litchis
2 cups clear apple juice
  (no added sugar)
1/3 cup strained lime juice
2 tablespoons sugar
1 1/4 x 1 1/4 in. piece fresh ginger,
  peeled and thinly sliced
4 sheets gelatin (about 1/4 oz.)

mint leaves

Drain the syrup from the litchis and reserve 1 cup of the syrup. Discard the remaining syrup. Place the reserved syrup, apple juice, lime juice, sugar, and ginger in a saucepan. Bring to a boil, then reduce the heat and simmer for 5 minutes. Strain into a heatproof bowl.

Place the gelatin sheets in a bowl of cold water and soak for 2 minutes or until they soften. Squeeze out the excess water, then add to the syrup. Stir until the gelatin has completely dissolved. Leave to cool.

Pour 2 tablespoons of the gelatin mixture into each of six 1/2-cup stemmed wine glasses, and divide the litchis among the wine glasses. Refrigerate until the gelatin has set. Spoon the remaining gelatin over the fruit and refrigerate until set. Before serving, garnish with mint leaves.

Serves 6

Peaches poached in wine

4 just-ripe, yellow-fleshed peaches
2 cups dessert wine, such as
  Sauternes
¼ cup orange liqueur
1 cup sugar
1 cinnamon stick
1 vanilla bean, split
8 mint leaves

mascarpone cheese or crème fraîche

Cut a small cross in the base of each peach. Immerse the peaches in boiling water for 30 seconds, then drain and cool slightly. Peel off the skin, cut in half, and carefully remove the pits.

Place the wine, liqueur, sugar, cinnamon stick, and vanilla bean in a deep-sided frying pan large enough to hold the peach halves in a single layer. Heat the mixture, stirring, until the sugar dissolves. Bring to a boil, then reduce the heat and simmer for 5 minutes. Add the peaches to the pan and simmer for 4 minutes, turning them over halfway through. Remove with a slotted spoon and leave to cool. Continue to simmer the syrup for 6–8 minutes or until thick. Strain and set aside.

Arrange the peaches on a serving platter, cut-side up. Spoon the syrup over the top and garnish each half with a mint leaf. Serve the peaches warm or chilled, with a dollop of mascarpone or crème fraîche.

Serves 4

Lemon granita

1¼ cups lemon juice
1 tablespoon lemon zest
1 cup sugar

Place the lemon juice, lemon zest, and sugar in a small saucepan and stir over low heat for 5 minutes or until the sugar is dissolved. Remove from the heat and leave to cool.

Add 2 cups water to the juice mixture and mix together well. Pour the mixture into a shallow 12 x 8 in. metal tray and place in the freezer until the mixture is beginning to freeze around the edges. Scrape the frozen sections back into the mixture with a fork. Repeat every 30 minutes until the mixture has even-sized ice crystals. Beat the mixture with a fork just before serving. To serve, spoon the lemon granita into six chilled glasses.

Serves 6

Panna cotta with blueberry compote

1 1/4 cups low-fat milk
1 vanilla bean, halved
1 cinnamon stick
1/2 teaspoon vanilla extract
1 tablespoon sugar
2 sheets gelatin
1 cup plain yogurt

Blueberry compote
1 cup fresh blueberries
1 tablespoon sugar
1/2 cup good-quality Marsala
1 cinnamon stick
1-in. strip lemon peel, white pith
   removed
1 vanilla bean, halved
1/2 teaspoon arrowroot

Pour the milk into a heavy-based saucepan. Scrape in the seeds from the vanilla bean and add the pod, cinnamon stick, vanilla extract, and the sugar. Bring to a boil, stirring, then remove from the heat and leave to infuse for 10 minutes.

Soak the gelatin in cold water for 5 minutes or until soft. Squeeze out and add the leaves to the milk. Stir over low heat until the leaves dissolve (do not boil). Remove the vanilla pod and the cinnamon stick. Cool to room temperature. Whisk in the yogurt. Pour into four 1/2-cup ramekins and chill for 6 hours or until set.

Place the berries in a saucepan and add the sugar, Marsala, cinnamon stick, and peel. Scrape in the seeds from the vanilla bean and add the pod. Cook over low heat for 15 minutes, stirring occasionally. Make sure the fruit does not break up. Mix the arrowroot with 2 teaspoons water and add to the fruit. Cook, stirring, until the mixture thickens. Leave to cool for at least 2 hours.

Run a knife around the edge of each ramekin and invert the panna cotta onto plates. Remove the cinnamon, peel, and pod from the compote and serve with the panna cotta.

Serves 4

Chocolate mousse

3½ oz. dark chocolate
¼ cup evaporated skim milk
2 tablespoons cocoa powder
¼ teaspoon rosewater extract or
  2 teaspoons vanilla extract
½ cup sugar
3 egg whites
cocoa powder, to dust

savoiardi (sponge finger cookies)

Chop the chocolate into small, even pieces and place in a heatproof bowl with the milk and cocoa powder. Bring a saucepan of water to a boil, then reduce the heat to a gentle simmer. Place the bowl over the saucepan, making sure the base of the bowl does not touch the water. Stir once, if necessary, to ensure even melting. When completely melted, mix until smooth, then stir in the rosewater or vanilla extract and leave to cool.

Place the sugar and ⅓ cup water in a small, heavy-based saucepan and stir over low heat until the sugar has dissolved. Bring to a simmer, without stirring, for 5 minutes or until a small amount of the syrup placed in a saucer of water forms a soft ball. Remove from the heat.

Meanwhile, using electric beaters, beat the egg whites in a clean, dry bowl until soft peaks form. With the beater on medium, gradually add the hot sugar syrup, then beat on high speed for 3–4 minutes or until the meringue is very thick and glossy. Gently fold in the cooled chocolate mixture, then pour into four ¾-cup serving glasses. Chill for at least 4 hours. Dust with cocoa and serve with a sponge finger cookie.

Serves 4

Drinks

Earl Grey summer tea

1 cinnamon stick
1 tablespoon Earl Grey tea leaves
1 cup orange juice
2 teaspoons finely grated orange zest
2 tablespoons sugar, or to taste
ice cubes
1 orange, sliced into thin rounds

4 cinnamon sticks

Place the cinnamon stick, tea leaves, orange juice, orange zest, and 3 cups water in a medium saucepan.

Slowly bring to a simmer over low heat. Once simmering, stir in the sugar, to taste, and stir until dissolved. Remove from the heat and allow to cool. Once the mixture has cooled, strain the liquid into a jar and refrigerate until cold.

Serve in a glass with lots of ice cubes and garnish with the orange slices and an extra cinnamon stick.

Makes four 8-oz. servings

Lemon, lime, and soda with citrus ice cubes

1 lemon
1 lime
2½ tablespoons lemon juice
⅔ cup lime juice cordial
2½ cups soda water, chilled

Using a sharp knife, remove the peel and white pith from the lemon and lime. On a chopping board, cut between the membranes to release the segments. Place a lemon and lime segment in each hole of an ice cube tray and cover with water. Freeze for 2–3 hours or overnight until firm.

Combine the lemon juice, lime juice cordial, and soda water.

Pour into long, chilled glasses with the ice cubes.

Makes two 12-oz. servings and 8 ice cubes

Passion fruit and vanilla ice cream whip

4 passion fruit
½ cup passion fruit yogurt
2 cups milk
1 tablespoon sugar
2 scoops vanilla ice cream

Scoop out the pulp from the passion fruit and push through a sieve to remove the seeds. Place in a blender with the yogurt, milk, sugar, and ice cream and blend until smooth.

Pour into tall glasses and serve with an extra scoop of ice cream, if desired.

Makes two 12-oz. servings

Melon shake

1 lb. honeydew melon, peeled and
   seeded
2 tablespoons honey
1½ cups milk
5 scoops vanilla ice cream

ground nutmeg

Cut the honeydew melon into 1-in.
pieces and place in a blender. Mix
for 30 seconds or until smooth.

Add the honey, milk, and ice cream
and blend the mixture for another
10–20 seconds or until well combined
and smooth. Serve sprinkled with
nutmeg.

Makes two 12-oz. servings

Coconut and lime lassi

1 ½ cups coconut milk
¾ cup plain yogurt
¼ cup lime juice
¼ cup sugar
8–10 ice cubes

lime slices

Blend together the coconut milk, yogurt, lime juice, sugar, and ice cubes until the mixture is well combined and the ice cubes are well crushed.

Pour into tall glasses and serve immediately, garnished with slices of fresh lime.

Makes two 12-oz. servings

Peachy eggnog

2 eggs, separated
1/4 cup milk
1/4 cup sugar
1/3 cup cream
1 3/4 cups peach nectar
2 tablespoons orange juice

ground nutmeg

Beat the egg yolks, milk, and half the sugar in a bowl and place over a pan of simmering water—do not allow the base of the bowl to touch the water. Cook, stirring, for 8 minutes or until the custard thickens. Remove from the heat and cover the surface with plastic wrap. Allow to cool.

Beat the egg whites until frothy. Add the remaining sugar, to taste, then beat until stiff peaks form. In a separate bowl, whip the cream until soft peaks form.

Gently fold the egg whites and cream into the cooled custard. Stir in the nectar and juice. Cover and chill for 2 hours.

Beat the mixture lightly, pour into glasses, and sprinkle with nutmeg.

Makes four 8-oz. servings

Cranberry and vanilla ice cream spider

2 cups cranberry juice
2 cups soda water
4 scoops vanilla ice cream
$3/4$ cup cream
1 tablespoon sugar
$1/4$ cup flaked almonds, toasted

Combine the juice and soda water in a jar. Add a scoop of ice cream to each tall glass. Pour the juice and soda over the ice cream.

Whip the cream and sugar until soft peaks form. Spoon over the juice and soda and top with a sprinkle of almonds.

Makes four 8-oz. servings

Summer buttermilk smoothie

1½-lb. honeydew melon
2 peaches, peeled and sliced
1 cup strawberries, roughly chopped
4 mint leaves
½ cup buttermilk
½ cup orange juice
1–2 tablespoons honey

Remove the zest and seeds from the melon and cut the flesh into pieces.

Place the melon, peaches, strawberries, and mint leaves in a blender and blend until smooth.

Add the buttermilk, orange juice, and 1 tablespoon of the honey and blend to combine. Taste for sweetness and add more honey if needed.

Makes two 12-oz. servings

Note: This drink should be consumed within 3 hours of being made or it will lose its color and freshness of flavor.

Black currant crush

3 cups apple and black currant juice
2 cups soda water
1 tablespoon sugar
1 cup blueberries
ice cubes

Place the apple and black currant juice, soda water, sugar, and blueberries into a blender and blend until smooth.

Serve in chilled glasses over ice.

Makes four 10-oz. servings

Note: If you have a really good blender, you may wish to add the ice cubes when blending the other ingredients to make a smoothie.

Apricot whip

½ cup dried apricots
½ cup apricot yogurt
⅔ cup light coconut milk
1¼ cups milk
1 tablespoon honey
1 scoop vanilla ice cream

flaked coconut, toasted

Cover the apricots with boiling water and soak for 15 minutes. Drain and roughly chop. Place the apricots, yogurt, coconut milk, milk, honey, and ice cream in a blender and blend until smooth.

Pour into tall, chilled glasses and sprinkle with the flaked coconut.

Makes three 8-oz. servings

Chocoholic milk shake

½ cup cold milk
2 oz. dark chocolate, grated
2 tablespoons chocolate syrup
2 tablespoons cream
4 scoops chocolate ice cream
2 scoops chocolate ice cream, extra

grated dark chocolate

Blend the milk, chocolate, syrup, cream, and ice cream in a blender until smooth.

Pour into chilled glasses. Top each glass with a scoop of ice cream and sprinkle with grated chocolate.

Makes two 8-oz. servings

Banana-date smoothie

1 cup low-fat plain yogurt
½ cup skim milk
½ cup fresh dates, pitted and
    chopped
2 bananas, sliced
8 ice cubes

Place the yogurt, milk, dates, banana, and ice cubes in a blender. Blend until the mixture is smooth and the ice cubes have been well incorporated.

Serve in chilled glasses.

Makes two 12-oz. servings

Orange and cardamom herbal tea

3 cardamom pods
1 cup orange juice
3 strips orange zest
2 tablespoons sugar

Place the cardamom pods on a chopping board and press with the side of a large knife to crack them open. Place the cardamom, orange juice, zest, sugar, and 2 cups water in a pan and stir over medium heat for 10 minutes or until the sugar has dissolved. Bring to a boil, then remove from the heat.

Leave to infuse for 2–3 hours or until cool. Chill in the refrigerator. Strain and serve over ice.

Makes two 10-oz. servings

Virgin Mary

3 cups tomato juice
2 tablespoons lemon juice
1 tablespoon Worcestershire sauce
$\frac{1}{4}$ teaspoon ground nutmeg
few drops hot pepper sauce
1 cup ice (12 ice cubes)
2 lemon slices, halved

Place the tomato juice, lemon juice, Worcestershire sauce, nutmeg, and hot pepper sauce in a large jar and stir until combined.

Place the ice cubes in a blender and blend for 30 seconds or until the ice is crushed down to $\frac{1}{2}$ cup.

Pour the tomato juice mixture into serving glasses and add the crushed ice and lemon slices. Season with salt and pepper before serving.

Makes four 8-oz. servings

Mandarin and mango chill

1 mango, cut into slices
2 cups mandarin juice
½ cup lime juice cordial
1½ cups soda water
2 tablespoons sugar
ice cubes

Freeze the mango for about 1 hour or until semifrozen.

Combine the juice, cordial, soda water, and sugar in a jar.

Place the mango slices and some ice cubes into each glass, then pour in the juice mix.

Makes two 12-oz. servings

Very berry

1 cup low-fat strawberry yogurt
1/2 cup cranberry juice, chilled
1 cup strawberries, hulled and
   quartered
1 cup frozen raspberries

Combine the yogurt and cranberry juice in a blender. Add the quartered strawberries and two thirds of the raspberries. Blend until smooth.

Pour into chilled glasses and top with the remaining frozen raspberries. Serve with a spoon, as it is thick.

Makes four 8-oz. servings

Summer strawberry smoothie

1 tablespoon strawberry flavoring
1 cup mixed berry yogurt
1 cup strawberries, hulled
4 scoops frozen strawberry yogurt
few drops vanilla extract
ice cubes

Combine the strawberry flavoring, yogurt, strawberries, frozen yogurt, and vanilla in a blender and process until smooth.

Pour over lots of ice to serve.

Makes two 10-oz. servings

Big bold banana

3 cups soy milk, chilled
4 oz. soft silken tofu
4 very ripe bananas, sliced
1 tablespoon honey
1 tablespoon vanilla extract
1 tablespoon cocoa powder

Combine the soy milk and tofu in a blender. Add the banana, honey, vanilla extract, and cocoa powder. Blend until smooth.

Serve in tall, chilled glasses with a long spoon.

Makes four 12-oz. servings

Orange and ginger tea cooler

1 small orange
½–1 tablespoon Darjeeling tea leaves
1 cup ginger ale
8 thin slices glacé ginger
2 tablespoons sugar
4–6 ice cubes

mint leaves

Remove the peel from the orange using a vegetable peeler, avoiding the white pith, and cut into long, thin strips. Place half the peel and the tea leaves in a bowl and pour in 2 cups boiling water. Cover and leave to steep for 5 minutes, then strain through a fine strainer.

Pour into a jar, add the ginger ale, and chill for 6 hours or overnight if possible.

One hour before serving, add the ginger, sugar, and remaining orange peel. Stir well.

Pour into tall glasses, add 2–3 ice cubes per glass, and garnish with mint leaves.

Makes two 12-oz. servings

Lemon barley water

½ cup pearl barley
3 lemons
½ cup sugar
crushed ice

lemon slices

Wash the barley well and place in a medium pan. Using a sharp vegetable peeler, remove the peel from the lemons, avoiding the bitter white pith. Squeeze out the juice and set aside. Add the peel and 7 cups cold water to the barley and bring to a boil. Simmer briskly for 30 minutes. Add the sugar and mix to dissolve. Allow to cool.

Strain the liquid into a jar and add the lemon juice. Serve over crushed ice and garnish with lemon slices.

Makes four 8-oz. servings

Homemade lemonade

2³/₄ cups lemon juice
1¹/₄ cups sugar
ice cubes

mint leaves

Combine the lemon juice and sugar in a large bowl, stirring until the sugar has dissolved. Pour into a large jar.

Add 5 cups water to the jar, stirring well to combine. Chill.

To serve, pour over ice cubes and garnish with mint leaves.

Makes six 12-oz. servings

Banana passion

3 passion fruit, halved
1 large banana, chopped
1 cup skim milk
¼ cup low-fat plain yogurt

Scoop out the passion fruit pulp and place in a blender. Add the banana, milk, and yogurt and blend, turning quickly on and off (or use the pulse button), until smooth and the seeds are finely chopped. Add more milk if it is too thick. Don't blend for too long or it will become very bubbly and increase in volume.

Makes two 8-oz. servings

Smoothberry

1 1/2 cups strawberries, hulled
1/2 cup raspberries
1 1/2 cups boysenberries
1 cup milk
3 scoops vanilla ice cream

Place the strawberries, raspberries, boysenberries, milk, and ice cream in a blender and blend until smooth, then chill.

Pour into chilled glasses and serve.

Makes four 8-oz. servings

Note: If boysenberries are unavailable, any other berry can be used.

Iced chocolate

2 tablespoons rich chocolate topping
1 1/2 cups ice-cold milk
1 scoop vanilla ice cream

whipped cream
cocoa powder

Pour the chocolate topping into a glass and swirl it around the sides. Fill with the cold milk and add the ice cream.

Serve with a big swirl of whipped cream and dust with cocoa powder.

Makes one 12-oz. serving

Lemongrass tea

3 stalks lemongrass
2 slices lemon
3 teaspoons honey, or to taste

lemon slices

Prepare the lemongrass by removing the first two tough outer layers. For maximum flavor, only use the bottom third of the stalk (the white part). Slice thinly into rings. You could use the remaining stalks as a garnish, if you like.

Place the lemongrass in a jar and cover with 2½ cups boiling water. Add the lemon slices and cover. Allow to infuse and cool. When cooled to room temperature, strain. Add the honey to taste. Place the tea in the refrigerator to chill.

To serve, pour the tea into two glasses with extra slices of lemon. Add ice, if desired.

Makes two 10-oz. servings

Raspberry lemonade

2½ cups fresh or frozen raspberries,
  thawed
1¼ cups sugar
2 cups lemon juice
ice cubes

mint leaves

Combine the raspberries and sugar
in a blender and blend until smooth.

Place a strong sieve over a large
bowl and push the mixture through to
remove the seeds. Discard the seeds.

Add the lemon juice and mix well.
Pour into a large jar and stir in 6 cups
water, then chill.

To serve, pour over ice cubes and
garnish with mint leaves.

Makes six 12-oz. servings

Coconut and passion fruit smoothie

½ cup coconut milk
1 cup milk
¼ cup flaked coconut
¼ teaspoon natural vanilla extract
3 scoops vanilla ice cream
6-oz. can passion fruit pulp in syrup

Blend together the coconut milk, milk, coconut, vanilla, ice cream, and half the passion fruit pulp until the mixture is smooth and fluffy.

Stir in the remaining pulp and serve immediately.

Makes two 12-oz. servings

Sports shake

2 cups cold milk
2 tablespoons honey
$\frac{1}{2}$ teaspoon vanilla extract
1 tablespoon wheat germ
1 medium banana, sliced

Blend the milk, honey, vanilla, wheat germ, and banana until smooth.

Chill well and serve.

Makes two 8-oz. servings

Iced mint tea

4 peppermint tea bags
⅓ cup honey
2 cups grapefruit juice
1 cup orange juice

mint sprigs

Place the tea bags in a large, heatproof jar and pour in 3 cups boiling water. Allow to steep for 3 minutes, then remove and discard the bags. Stir in the honey and allow to cool.

Add the grapefruit and orange juices. Cover and chill in the refrigerator. Serve in glasses, garnished with mint.

Makes six 8-oz. servings

Mint julep

1 cup mint leaves
1 tablespoon sugar
1 tablespoon lemon juice
1 cup pineapple juice
1 cup ginger ale
ice cubes

mint leaves

Roughly chop the mint leaves and place in a heatproof jar with the sugar. Using a wooden spoon, bruise the mint. Add the lemon juice, pineapple juice, and ½ cup boiling water. Mix well. Cover with plastic wrap and leave for 30 minutes.

Strain, then refrigerate until cold.

Just before serving, add the ginger ale and mix well. Serve in glasses over ice and garnish with mint leaves.

Makes two 10-oz. servings

Breakfast shake

1 cup fruit, such as passion fruit,
   mango, banana, peaches,
   strawberries, or blueberries
1 cup milk
2 teaspoons wheat germ
1 tablespoon honey
¼ cup vanilla yogurt
1 tablespoon malt powder

Blend all the ingredients in a
blender for 30–60 seconds or
until well combined.

Pour into chilled glasses and serve
immediately.

Makes two 12-oz. servings

American iced tea

4 Ceylon tea bags
2 tablespoons sugar
2 tablespoons lemon juice
1½ cups dark grape juice
2 cups orange juice
1½ cups ginger ale
ice cubes

lemon slices

Place the tea bags in a heatproof bowl with 4 cups boiling water. Leave for 3 minutes. Remove the bags and stir in the sugar. Allow to cool.

Stir in the juices. Refrigerate until cold, then add the ginger ale. Serve over ice cubes with a slice of lemon.

Makes four 8-oz. servings

Cinnamon and custard shake

1½ cups milk
¾ cup prepared custard
3 teaspoons honey
1½ teaspoons ground cinnamon
3 scoops vanilla ice cream

ground cinnamon

Blend together the milk, custard, honey, cinnamon, and ice cream until smooth and fluffy.

Pour the shake into tall glasses, sprinkle with the extra cinnamon, and serve immediately.

Makes two 12-oz. servings

Chocolate-cherry smoothie

2 cups milk
1/4 cup whole, red glacé cherries
1/4 cup dried coconut
1 tablespoon chocolate topping
3 scoops chocolate ice cream

Blend together the milk, cherries, coconut, topping, and ice cream until smooth and fluffy.

Pour into tall glasses and serve immediately.

Makes two 12-oz. servings

Index

INDEX

Photographers: Jon Bader, Craig Cranko, Joe Filshie, Scott Hawkins, Ian Hofstetter, Andre Martin, Rob Reichenfeld, Brett Stevens, Jon Paul Urizar

Food stylists: Anna-Marie Bruechert, Marie-Hélène Clauzon, Jane Collins, Sarah de Nardi, Georgina Dolling, Carolyn Fienberg, Cherise Koch, Michelle Norianto, Sarah O'Brien, Sally Parker, Maria Villegas

Food preparation: Alison Adams, Valli Little, Tracey Meharg, Kerrie Mullins, Briget Palmer, Kim Passenger, Justine Poole, Christine Sheppard, Angela Tregonning

Special thanks to Wheel & Barrow, Sydney, Australia, for supplying props and accessories for the cover and chapter openers.

 **Laurel Glen Publishing**

An imprint of the Advantage Publishers Group
5880 Oberlin Drive, San Diego, CA 92121-4794
www.laurelglenbooks.com

All notations of errors or omissions should be addressed to Laurel Glen Publishing, Editorial Department,
at the above address. All other correspondence (author inquiries, permissions, and rights) concerning the
content of this book should be addressed to Murdoch Books® a division of Murdoch Magazines Pty Ltd,
GPO Box 1203, Sydney NSW 1045, Australia.

NOTE: Those who might be at risk from the effects of salmonella poisoning (the elderly, pregnant women,
young children, and those with a compromised immune system) should consult their physician before
trying recipes made with raw eggs.

Library of Congress Cataloging-in-Publication Data
Cool food / [editor: Katharine Gasparini]
     p. cm.
     Includes index.
     ISBN 1-57145-495-0
     1. Quick and easy cookery. I. Gasparini, Katharine.
  TX833.5 .C663 2003
  641.5'55--dc21   2002190818

Printed by Tien Wah Press, Singapore
1 2 3 4 5   07 06 05 04 03

Editorial Director: Diana Hill Editor: Katharine Gasparini
U.S. Editor: Kerry MacKenzie Creative Director: Marylouise Brammer
Designer: Wing Ping Tong Food Director: Lulu Grimes
Photographer (chapter openers): Ian Hofstetter
Stylist (chapter openers): Cherise Koch
Picture Librarian: Mary Ferizis
Chief Executive: Juliet Rogers
Publisher: Kay Scarlett
Production Manager: Kylie Kirkwood

Front cover: Penne with shrimp, page 178
Back cover: Crab salad with green mango and coconut, page 128